"Paul is living proof that you can be wildly successful in business while leading by inspiration, not intimidation. It's refreshing to see the magic tools to success start with the simple act of taking care of your people."

JIM NANTZ, *Commentator and Sports Personality*

"Paul has captured the subtle yet complex interplay between strategy and systematic execution in a practical and impactful way. His incredible vision, deep understanding of organizations and people and lessons learned from experience have given us a great playbook for developing impeccable organizational hygiene. I deeply respect the grit and determination that has led the Insperity senior team to build not only a world class company but also pioneer an entire industry. BoyarMiller is a much better organization because of our relationship with Insperity and I am blessed to call Paul a friend. We will be even better as we apply the lessons and guidance so humbly shared in *Take Care of Your People*."

BILL BOYAR, *Founding Shareholder, BoyarMiller*

"Do you know what your 'people policy' is—Paul Sarvadi's book is a valuable read on what matters most in an organization viz. the strength of its human capital. Offering words of wisdom infused with a common sense approach that comes from leading a company that has repeatedly demonstrated its ability to be a 'top 100 workplace', the book offers valuable suggestions on growing a sustainable organizational culture, goal setting, building trust and an actionable approach to the idea of servant leadership."

LATHA RAMCHAND, *Provost and Executive Vice Chancellor for Academic Affairs, University of Missouri*

TAKE CARE OF YOUR PEOPLE

PAUL SARVADI

TAKE CARE
of your
PEOPLE

**THE ENLIGHTENED CEO'S GUIDE
TO BUSINESS SUCCESS**

ForbesBooks

Published by ForbesBooks, Charleston, South Carolina.
Member of Advantage Media Group.

ForbesBooks is a registered trademark, and the ForbesBooks colophon is a trademark of Forbes Media, LLC.

Printed in the United States of America.

10 9 8 7 6 5 4 3 2

ISBN: 978-1-946633-67-5
LCCN: 2018964385

Cover design by Chris Nowak.
Layout design by Megan Elger.

This publication is designed to provide accurate and authoritative information in regard to the subject matter covered. It is sold with the understanding that the publisher is not engaged in rendering legal, accounting, or other professional services. If legal advice or other expert assistance is required, the services of a competent professional person should be sought.

Advantage Media Group is proud to be a part of the Tree Neutral® program. Tree Neutral offsets the number of trees consumed in the production and printing of this book by taking proactive steps such as planting trees in direct proportion to the number of trees used to print books. To learn more about Tree Neutral, please visit **www.treeneutral.com**.

Since 1917, the Forbes mission has remained constant. Global Champions of Entrepreneurial Capitalism. ForbesBooks exists to further that aim by bringing the Stories, Passion, and Knowledge of top thought leaders to the forefront. ForbesBooks brings you The Best in Business. To be considered for publication, please visit **www.forbesbooks.com**.

*This book is dedicated to Richard Rawson, Steve Arizpe,
and Jay Mincks, my partners and friends who have been on a covenant
walk with me building Insperity, overcoming the challenges,
and learning and applying the concepts in this book.*

*And to our wives Dr. Victoria Sarvadi, Dawn Rawson,
Charissa Arizpe, and Sally Mincks who shared the stewardship
of this vision and the faith to persevere.*

TABLE OF CONTENTS

FOREWORD

I've worked for several organizations of different sizes and types, and in many different roles. As I look back on my journey, I've come to realize there's one common thread that separates the great businesses from the good ones: the people behind them.

That's why I was thrilled when my friend Paul Sarvadi shared his book, *Take Care of Your People: An Enlightened CEO's Guide to Success*, with me. This book embodies all the things I value and put into practice when I was chairman and CEO of Yum! Brands, Inc., one of the world's largest restaurant companies, featuring Taco Bell, KFC, and Pizza Hut.

Like Paul, I've come to realize the power that people—employees—have over the success of a business. You have to build your people capability first. Only then can you satisfy customers and make money.

When Paul started Insperity, the well-being of his people was top of mind. He had a clear mission and vision for the culture he aspired to create. He saw the return that could come from investing in and supporting the people in his business, the businesses he served and the communities these businesses shaped. He didn't do it solely for personal success. He did it because he truly wanted to make a difference in the lives of his employees, clients, and community as a whole.

I wish more business owners started with this same approach. There is an absolute urgent need for more positive leadership, like Paul's, in the world.

Leadership is a privilege. As a leader, you have been given the ability to change lives. You were chosen to lead because at some point you demonstrated the skill, ability, and potential to guide and influence others. Your people are looking to you to help them succeed. It's your responsibility to coach them to be the best they can be.

In this book, Paul gives you a clear-cut road map—not just a general overview—of how to become a genuinely influential leader and build a people-first company. His ten strategies provide a true play-by-play of what you should know or do at every turn.

Since retiring from Yum! Brands, I have recently founded a leadership development company, OGOLead, based on teaching these very strategies. Like Insperity, we are mission driven: make the world a better place by developing better leaders. Servant leadership is at the core of what we believe. Our leaders are taught to engage, equip, and elevate their people, so they can rise to their full potential and consistently make a positive impact on the organization.

If you're like me, you have a million ideas for improving your business and developing your people. Great ideas, but putting them into action isn't always as straightforward. In this compelling read, Paul teaches you how to think strategically as well as systematically, to help you finally get your ideas off the ground.

It's not every day that you get clear, practical, proven advice like this, from someone who's been right where you are. There's a reason why his company has been voted among the best places to work nationwide more than 146 times—and the number-one best place to work in Houston, the fourth largest city in the country, four years in a row.

I would be remiss if I didn't say, even with lots of inspiration and determination, there were times when I wasn't sure about my journey to success. After all, I was just a kid who grew up in a trailer park (*many* trailer parks, actually) and worked his way up the ranks one job at a time.

The leadership hat can be a heavy one to bear, and it made me weary—especially since I had a group of people counting on me to make game-changing decisions and lead the way. I often questioned if I was doing the right thing, making the right choices. Was I good enough?

That's why Paul's tenth "bonus" strategy hit me the hardest. He hones in on the relentless conviction and faith you have to have in yourself, your mission, and your vision in order to succeed. This chapter is real. It's raw. It's Paul's heart and soul on paper.

I was incredibly moved. It really touched the core of how I felt so many times when my convictions were challenged and I had nothing but my faith to see me through. When it seems impossible to persevere (and it will at some point, trust me), cling to the advice in this chapter. It'll give you the power to push through even in the toughest times.

Use this book as your "North Star" or guiding light. *Take Care of Your People* will transform the way you look at your current business or shape the way you start a new one. Instead of focusing solely on areas such as sales and marketing, technology, finance, etc., you'll learn to focus on your people first. And that is, without a doubt, what matters most.

Everybody makes a difference. As business leaders, it's our duty to design a culture within our companies where everyone can be appreciated and recognized for the value they bring to the organization.

—David C. Novak

ACKNOWLEDGMENTS

I would like to thank several people for their contributions to this book. First, thanks to my wife, Dr. Victoria Sarvadi, who wrote an amazing book of her own and inspired me to complete this mission. She has always been my inspiration!

Thanks to Morlley Ware for working with me to form the foundation for this book many years ago and for patiently waiting to see this come to fruition. She did not labor in vain!

Thanks to Michael Levin for establishing an effective approach for the message of this book to reach my heroes: small- and medium-sized business owners and leaders. His professionalism and skill energized me to sharpen my message and find my voice, making this project a comfortable conversation with the community champions we strive to support at Insperity.

Thanks to Jalyn Noel for shepherding the process and dealing with the many details inherent in bringing a book to completion. She did a great job of gently cracking the whip to keep me on schedule. We would not have made it without her!

Thanks to the Insperity creative marketing team for their help, especially with the cover, and other Insperity experts I consulted along the way. I am blessed to be surrounded by truly gifted people.

Thanks to the team at Advantage|ForbesBooks for their hard work and professionalism. They brought great energy and expertise to the table.

A special thanks to all of the employees of Insperity. They are the guardians of our mission-driven culture and demonstrate daily what an effective people strategy can produce. I am proud and humbled to lead them as we help businesses succeed so communities can prosper.

CHAPTER ONE

Take Care of Your People

As a small- or medium-sized business (SMB), you face many obstacles. Some days, it probably seems like the minute one problem is solved, another rears its ugly head. And as the captain of the ship, all the responsibility falls on you.

I know, because I was there too once—contending with a never-ending string of crises, challenges, setbacks, and upheavals as I worked to get my incipient business off the ground. But from the very start, I always knew there was one thing, above all else, that we would have to get right in order to thrive: our staff—our human capital. I have been at the helm from the startup phase to CEO of a publicly traded company with several thousand employees. The common thread through every stage is, the people make the difference. That's your guiding light, your North Star

This book will teach you how to take care of your people, because when you get that right, everything else falls into place.

that will keep propelling you toward greatness, even when nothing else seems to be going your way.

This book will teach you how to take care of your people, because when you get that right, everything else falls into place.

At Insperity, the company I co-founded in 1986, we understand the demands of human capital management better than anyone; after all, we practically invented the HR-outsourcing industry to help SMB owners like yourself. Payroll, hiring, terminating employees, performance management, benefits, legal compliance: the administrative tasks a business owner must contend with are numerous, varied, and constantly in flux. It's a full-time job to keep up with all of it; in fact, it's much more than a single full-time job. You need a dedicated team of professionals to really handle it. For a small- or medium-sized business owner—whether you're an upstart first-time entrepreneur or a decades-long veteran—dealing with all this stuff can leave you feeling overwhelmed, drowning in an alphabet soup of acronymic regulations, personnel paperwork, and administrivia.

The velocity of business has changed. Information zips around at the speed of light. In days gone by, we could control messaging more easily, framing it carefully as it cascaded down layer by layer within an organization. Now, information seems to move along one flat and frenetic plane, where a thousand people already know about a new development or change in the market before you even have a chance to respond to it. That's not a problem in and of itself; it just means we need a more innovative, thoughtful approach to HR that keeps us ahead of the curve.

Our approach is simple: we allow companies to succeed by taking care of the things that might distract you from the bigger picture, helping you control expenses, minimize risk exposure, and maximize your opportunities for revenue generation. But nobody can really take care of your people if *you're* not doing everything you can do to take care of them in the first place. I know how hard it can be. It's taken me decades to learn the secrets of how to do it right.

And now I want to share those secrets with you.

The Human Capital Strategy Multiplier

There are five major strategic areas that are key to any organization's success: sales, finance, operations, technology, and human capital. Most companies effectively address only a few of these areas, but the most successful organizations manage all five.

In working with thousands of SMBs over the years, I've found that the most frequently neglected area is human capital—and that's unfortunate, because your *people* as a group are the most critical asset of your business.

It's understandable why this gets sidelined. Most business leaders are naturally inclined to focus on the other

> **The most frequently neglected area is human capital—and that's unfortunate, because your people as a group are the most critical asset of your business.**

areas, like sales and finance, that fall more in their entrepreneurial wheelhouse. The day-to-day demands of running a company; the urgency of resolving problems in sales, finance, operations, and technology; and the strategic precedence of the sexier, flashier, and more engaging strategic areas divert attention from HR concerns. For entrepreneurs, human capital sometimes seems like the fifth wheel or the ugly stepchild of commerce; everyone knows it's there, but no one quite knows what to do with it. Or even wants to deal with it.

But relegating human capital management to the back burner can be detrimental to a company's success, since a well-rounded human capital strategy is not just an administrative necessity; it's central to growth. It allows a company to run better, grow faster and make more money. It enables you to attract and hire the right people, retain and develop key talent, reward and maintain top performers, and effectively lead them.

Since a well-rounded human capital strategy is not just an administrative necessity; it's central to growth.

Furthermore, a strong human capital strategy elevates each of the other four elements, a fact that underscores its dynamic and pivotal role within a smoothly running enterprise.

Sales, finance, operations, and technology all need human capital to thrive. They all depend on having the right people in the right places doing the right things.

Sales, finance, operations, and technology all need human capital to thrive. They all depend on having the right people in the right places doing the right things.

There's a wealth of empirical data that supports this claim, too. The following chart contains information from a study conducted over several years by three college professors and published in *The HR Scorecard: Linking People, Strategy, and Performance*. This chart measures the performance of 429 public companies. The companies in the top 10 percent of strategic HR practices perform better (in terms of sales per employee and market value) than those in the bottom 10 percent of HR rankings. This shows the dramatic impact of a sound human capital strategy.

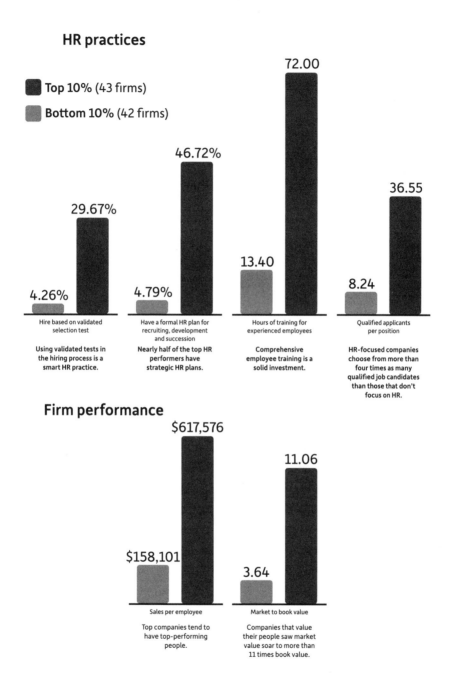

HR practices

Top 10% (43 firms)
Bottom 10% (42 firms)

4.26% / 29.67%	4.79% / 46.72%	13.40 / 72.00	8.24 / 36.55

Hire based on validated selection test

Have a formal HR plan for recruiting, development and succession

Hours of training for experienced employees

Qualified applicants per position

Using validated tests in the hiring process is a smart HR practice.

Nearly half of the top HR performers have strategic HR plans.

Comprehensive employee training is a solid investment.

HR-focused companies choose from more than four times as many qualified job candidates than those that don't focus on HR.

Firm performance

$158,101 / $617,576

3.64 / 11.06

Sales per employee

Market to book value

Top companies tend to have top-performing people.

Companies that value their people saw market value soar to more than 11 times book value.

Source: Brian E. Becker, Mark A. Huselid, and Dave Ulrich, *The HR Scorecard: Linking People, Strategy, and Performance* (Boston: Harvard Business Press, 2001), 16-17.

Some of the most successful companies (or those that are in their prime growth phase), such as Google, Apple, Marriott International, Southwest Airlines, and General Mills, have been led by visionary leaders who understand the important role that people play in the success of the organization. Companies included on *Fortune* magazine's "100 Best Companies to Work For" list typically have one common denominator—a strong human capital strategy.[1] That strategy provides a firm with an organizational cohesion that is flexible enough to allow for evolution and change, but strong and sturdy enough to provide long-term consistency, reliability, and guidance.

Put simply, people will make—or break—an organization. And if you as the company head can't understand what makes people tick, you won't be able to get a handle on things, even when enlisting outside help from a company like ours. The CEO wears many hats, and one of the most important is the "behavioral scientist" hat. You must have an intuitive understanding of what motivates people. What compels them to do well—or causes them to fail. How to inspire them to work for a common cause, day in, day out, with a clear understanding of their roles within the organization.

This is perhaps the hardest part of the job. Human relations are complicated because *human nature* is complicated. Even after all these years in the business, people continue to surprise me. Each day, I learn something new about human nature, encounter new challenges in human capital management that I haven't dealt with before. People are complex and dynamic beings. You can try to fight it—or you can understand it and use it to your advantage.

When you finally *get* it, you'll find that everything clicks into place. Your people will work for you because they *enjoy* it. They'll

---

1   "100 Best Companies to Work For," *Fortune*, accessed November 5, 2018, http://fortune.com/best-companies/.

fulfill their responsibilities not because they "have" to, but because they "get to." They'll produce "discretionary effort," that coveted going-above-and-beyond kind of performance that eludes so many workplaces where the CEO doesn't know his people, doesn't understand what lights a fire inside them.

What we're talking about here is alignment. One of the most important hats the entrepreneur puts on each day (and I do mean *each* day) is the "alignment hat." It underpins everything you do as part of your human capital strategy.

As we help business leaders assess their companies, we often find that the goals are misaligned. For example, although the CEO and executive team may have a clear understanding of the company's culture, the rest of the company—key leaders and employees—do not have the same perception. Alignment is essential for all aspects of the human capital strategy, including the company's mission, goals, and objectives; job roles and expectations—everything. When one or several areas are disconnected, the entire organization is at risk.

And speaking of risk, the risk associated with personnel issues is enormous. Each employee—from the moment an application is completed until seven years after a termination—represents a level of employment risk under the laws and regulations with which every business owner must comply. Failure to meet the myriad and mercurial legal obligations can lead to fines, penalties, bankruptcy, and even, in extreme cases, litigation or criminal prosecution. Handling all that is a tall order for anyone, much less a busy executive juggling a hundred other tasks at once to keep the ship on course.

This book will help you take a closer look at your company in order to uncover which components of your human capital strategy are missing or broken, and how you can improve them.

I have stood where you stand. I know the pressures you face, the time you lack, and the fear you have of making changes that might result in lost productivity or the departure of valued employees. This book will help you take a closer look at your company in order to uncover which components of your human capital strategy are missing or broken, and how you can improve them. It will allow you to assess the strengths and weaknesses of your strategy, pinpointing what you're doing right while identifying areas for improvement, en route to building your own comprehensive human capital strategy custom to your business.

CHAPTER TWO

Ten Strategies (and Decades of Wisdom)

In 1986, my business partner Jerry McIntosh and I started a company with three clients, two desks, and one phone with a *really* long cord. We weathered many trials and tribulations, picked ourselves back up when we were knocked down, learned what to do (and what not to do), and were fortunate to enjoy many successes along the way. As a result, I have great respect and appreciation for those who choose to take the entrepreneurial journey, because I *know* what it's like to start your own business. I've endured the difficult sacrifices that owning a business requires: taking everything you have saved, borrowing all you can, and dumping everything, including yourself, into your vision. In return, you get to work sixteen-hour days, reinvest every nickel and dime you make over the next few years, and contend with a perpetual, nagging fear that maybe none of this is going to work out.

But take it from me—eventually (hopefully), your commitment and perseverance will pay off. Today, I smile when I reminisce about our early struggles. Since then, Insperity has grown to an internationally respected powerhouse, employing 3,100 people in more than 70 locations across the United States. We serve more than 100,000 clients with a combined workforce of two million employees. As a trusted advisor to America's best businesses, Insperity provides administrative relief, better benefits, reduced liabilities, a state-of-the-art HR-technology infrastructure, and a customized service plan for maximizing productivity and profitability—in short, big-business benefits for small- and medium-sized firms. Our business performance solutions help you better manage expenses and employee performance, control time and attendance costs, recruit and retain key talent, provide round-the-clock access to dependable technology, affordably insure the business, improve workforce alignment and productivity, and more.

With revenues of $3.3 billion, Insperity has continued to grow at a compound annual growth rate of more than 15 percent since its 1997 debut on the New York Stock Exchange (NYSE: NSP). We have also received over a hundred workplace-related awards throughout the country, including "Best Places to Work," "Best Places to Work For," and "Top 100 Workplaces." This includes four years in a row as the number one best place to work in Houston, Texas—the nation's fourth largest city and our hometown. Many of these awards are determined in large part by surveys of Insperity employees themselves. We don't just assist other companies with their human capital needs—we walk the walk too, providing a model for what a good "people policy" looks like.

If It Doesn't Exist, Create It Yourself

Imagine starting a company without an industry. When Insperity began, the concept of "HR outsourcing" was so novel, it was a challenge to even explain to people (including creditors and investors!) what we were doing. There was no successful competitor to learn from, no trade association to provide guidance—we didn't even know the right category in which to list ourselves in the phone book! Soon, we realized that we weren't merely founding a company, we were creating a new industry. Now *that's* a startup!

Jerry and I had to figure it all out by ourselves. Blazing a new trail all on our own was as exciting as it was daunting. But we never wavered. We knew how powerful Insperity's service offering was and the positive impact it could have on small- and medium-sized businesses.

We also knew that after our first attempt, working for another firm (prior to starting Insperity), went bankrupt, we had to take a different approach the next time—one that was more philosophical in nature, that really considered the foundational *values* of the company, not just how it would make money. Therefore, the development of Insperity's first business plan did not begin, as most business plans do, with cold, hard economics. Instead, it revolved around *people* and *values:*

> *What kind of company do we want to build?*
>
> *How would we want employees to describe our company?*
>
> *How can we turn a profit while living out our values every day?*

Just before Christmas in 1985, Jerry and I sat down one evening and talked through these questions. That conversation permanently altered the course of our lives. That night, the seed of a multibillion-dollar company was planted. Insperity was born out of the belief that regardless of how good our business ideas might be, or how hard we worked, the kind of company we'd create would be determined by *our human capital strategy*. Insperity's eventual success would be inextricably linked to the success of our *people*.

> **Regardless of how good our business ideas might be, or how hard we worked, the kind of company we'd create would be determined by our human capital strategy. Insperity's eventual success would be inextricably linked to the success of our people.**

With that guiding principle in mind, our focus shifted to fine-tuning our human capital approach:

What kind of employees do we want to hire?

How will we treat them?

How do we expect employees to treat each other?

What are our expectations about the way we treat our clients, vendors, and stakeholders?

The answers to these simple questions formed the philosophical foundation of the multibillion-dollar company that thrives today. And those questions are as relevant to us now as they were at the beginning. Everything starts, and ends, with your people.

Strategic vs. Systematic

Developing an effective human capital strategy requires both a *strategic* and a *systematic* approach to planning and implementation. What's the difference between the two? The strategic side is more creative and subjective, and it focuses on the big picture, whereas the systematic side is more logical and objective, emphasizing the parts or the details. Strategic thinking is chiefly concerned with "concept," whereas systematic thinking centers on "execution." For example, strategic thinking might produce a great idea for a new business, product, or service, while systematic thinking generates the technical and logistical processes to realize it. Both approaches work hand in hand to produce great things.

Naturally, most people prefer one style of thinking over the other. But a successful human capital plan includes a mix of both styles. You can come up with a visionary new idea, but if it lacks the processes or systems to implement it, nothing will come of it. The same can happen when a systematic process or technology is developed independent of strategy; if that process or technology is disconnected from a broader goal or vision, it simply does not serve a purpose.

Engaging in strategic and systematic thinking together produces a more complete, more effective human capital plan, one where the strategic and systematic elements function symbiotically, strengthening and reinforcing each other. This is not just theoretical verbiage that sounds nice in a business book; it's a proven and practical approach that has strengthened our organization and the thousands of businesses we've supported for more than thirty years, and it's a theme we'll come back to many times in the following chapters.

A Common Language

An effective HR strategy that really takes care of your people covers all three levels of HR activity. The base level of HR is the administration layer, which is transaction driven. This layer includes meeting responsibility for the sensitive data and information you keep on your staff, and compliance with laws and regulations required as an employer. Complexity is the enemy in this layer coupled with the ongoing repetitive nature of payroll and government reporting.

The second level of HR is the process layer, which is event driven. Hiring, firing, enrolling in benefits, changes to employees' pay, benefits or job functions—all of these carry risk if processes are not properly identified and followed. For small- and medium-sized companies, this layer is the most problematic because of the wide variety of events driving this layer of HR activity happen randomly and consistent process management is seldom a strong point in small business.

The third level of HR is the strategic layer, which is outcome driven. This is when a company wants to achieve a specific outcome like lower turnover or increased sales or service results. This layer is where the highest level of understanding of HR practices and behavioral science meet to help a business achieve strategic objectives.

Three Levels of an Effective HR Strategy

Strategic
Outcome Driven

Process
Event Driven

Administration
Transaction Driven

An effective HR strategy will address all three layers with strategic and systematic thinking combining HR technology and HR expertise in a "software with a service" model. Each specific HR strategy will be developed and executed with the one overarching goal of demonstrating to your people you really care about them.

Ten Strategies to Launch You into the Stratosphere

In each of the following chapters, I'm going to show you specific solutions you can implement today—ten core human capital strategies that will enable you to soar past your competitors:

Strategy #1 is "Getting your culture right." Whether your corporate culture is created by design or evolves naturally on its own, it's really the foundation for everything else.

Strategy #2 concerns "Finding, hiring, and keeping the best"—techniques for recruiting and retention that turn your workforce into a team of all-stars who gel with one another and support the organization's culture.

Strategy #3 deals with the thorny issue of compensation and rewards—how to keep your people happy with their salary and benefits and figuring out who should be paid what so that you can attract top talent without busting your budget.

Strategy #4 is a "playing-defense" strategy—protecting yourself and the company from damaging lawsuits and legal claims while ensuring compliance with an ever-changing bevy of regulations.

Strategy #5 is about "knowledge rightly applied"—getting the most out of your workforce by optimizing performance reviews, training, and professional development.

Strategy #6 teaches how to "turn bureaucracy into high performance" by harnessing the right HR technology in the right way.

Strategy #7 concerns an important but often-overlooked issue: if you're buying or selling a company, what do you need to know about the "people" issues before making the transaction?

Strategy #8 addresses organization and leadership strategy—even the best employees need a leader at the helm who can direct the company and ensure all the moving parts are running together.

Strategy #9 discusses communication strategies.

Strategy #10 is about "entrepreneurial conviction"—the value of having faith in yourself and what you're doing as you work to build something great.

CHAPTER THREE

Strategy #1: Getting Your Culture Right

Corporate culture is like the oil in an engine. It's not a mechanical component or moving part of the engine, but rather the lubricant that allows it to run smoothly and effectively. The culture sets the tone for the company, and it defines how the organization treats employees and how employees should act toward each other, the customers, vendors, and other stakeholders. Corporate culture affects every component of a human capital strategy, from the company's recruiting and selection of employees to performance management, compensation, and employer liability management.

Corporate culture—the organization's unique personality that influences behaviors and attitudes—is not just a touchy-feely concept about how good or bad employees feel, but rather a powerful driver of corporate success.

Every company has a corporate culture, whether it's by accident or by design. The culture is either purposefully and strategically developed by the leadership to support the company's mission, or it's left to chance and naturally evolves on its own. Whatever the case, the culture is a living, breathing thing that strongly impacts individual and corporate performance.

Your People Define Your Corporate Culture

At Insperity, we custom-built our corporate culture based on certain values that we wanted to embody—values that would not only be the foundation of a profitable business, but also create an environment that was pleasant to work in.

Though our culture was methodically designed by the leaders of the organization, it's still a two-way street that runs "bottom-up" as much as "top-down." Culture is not merely something executives create and then foist onto the workforce. It's really employees who shape the culture; in fact, there would be no culture without them. Employees define a company's culture by answering one simple question: "What is it like to work at this company?" If the answer isn't good, you have a problem.

Remember that corporate culture thrives on trust; after all, the culture is largely characterized by the relationship between the company and its people. A good culture encourages a deep level of confidence within each employee in knowing not just what to do, but also how and why to do it. This trust facilitates the alignment of personal goals with the vision of the company, allowing everyone to work together symbiotically.

Corporate Culture and Individual Effort

One reason corporate culture is so important is that it has a concrete impact on individual effort. When employees know what behaviors and actions are encouraged and rewarded by the organization, they develop a sense of emotional stability and feel comfortable to perform their roles without looking over their shoulders at every turn. In other words, a positive corporate culture enables employees to reach their full potential by cultivating confidence in themselves and their work.

Conversely, an emotionally draining or draconian culture has the opposite effect, making employees doubt themselves, mistrust their coworkers and supervisors, and go about their day unhappily or in fear of being reprimanded for the slightest oversight. That's bad for business: unhappy employees tend to make *unproductive* employees.

But when employees understand the expectations and are rewarded for following them, they can move freely without one foot on the gas and the other on the brake. This certainly propels any engine to perform better and faster.

Corporate Culture and Team Collaboration

A positive, well-defined, and supported corporate culture can also dramatically affect team performance for the same reasons. Emotional stability is even more critical in a group collaboration due to the natural dynamics and perceived risks team members recognize in a collective setting. The same individual doubt about making decisions that stems from a negative corporate culture is multiplied many times over in a group situation.

A negative corporate culture can give rise to Machiavellian politics, backbiting gossip, and indecisiveness. When people are unsure how and why decisions should be made, they feel unsafe and are less likely to stick their neck out. But when a group of talented people is presented with clear expectations, know their mission, and possess a firm understanding of the values of the organization, their innovative capacity is unleashed—they're free to do great things, knowing they're acting within an organizational culture that supports them.

An Extension of the Brand

Your corporate culture extends beyond employee morale and productivity. Ultimately, it's an extension of your brand; it affects your firm's reputation in the marketplace and the community. In a sense, the culture is the interface between the company and the world at large— the thing that links the "internal" environment of the business itself and the "external" presence of the company in the eyes of clients, collaborators, competitors, and the general public.

In other words, as the culture goes, so goes the brand. You can't put forward a good face to the world if your employees are miserable at work. Cultivating a healthy, positive culture "on the inside" will boost your organization's public stature and status. And as we'll discuss more in the following chapter, having a strong "employment brand"—being recognized as a great place to work—will draw top talent to your company.

Consider, for example, the well-known example of Southwest Airlines, which has built a culture—and a brand—that emphasizes light-hearted humor and fun as a fundamental part of the employee and consumer experience. Humor and fun are also essential qualities of our culture at Insperity. I'd go so far as to say that I don't think you can really build a positive and productive culture without making things fun on some level. We're an HR company that deals with very serious matters, but that doesn't mean that humor has no place. On the contrary—you need that jocularity in your culture to strike the right balance and keep people happy.

I know this aspect of it can get lost or overlooked, especially if you're at the top. Fun? Who has time for fun when you have half a dozen fires to put out by Tuesday. Everything falls on the shoulders of the CEO. Everyone's livelihood depends on how well you do your job. It is, needless to say, a sobering undertaking. But you need to allow yourself to have a good time, too. To laugh. To crack jokes. Your people look to you as a leader, and that doesn't just mean they take orders from you; it means they emulate your behavior as well. If they see you enjoying yourself at work, that enjoyment will be contagious.

Developing a Mission Statement and List of Core Values

Before "corporate culture" and "work-life balance" became buzzwords in corporate America, Jerry and I were already focused on creating an environment that would encourage high-octane productivity while keeping our employees satisfied—the sort of rare environment that would make us the envy of the business world.

If you're pursuing the "culture by design" track, then it should start with creating a mission statement and list of foundational values. In our company's early days, we toiled over and tweaked these statements until we felt they captured what we wanted to build. In the years since then, we have regularly revisited both our mission and values to assess the need for updates—but I guess we did it right the first time, since only twice have we altered the mission statement, and only once did we need to adjust the core values.

Insperity Mission Statement

Our mission is to help businesses succeed so communities prosper.

Insperity Values

- Integrity as the cornerstone of personal and corporate conduct.

- Respect for the worth of the individual.

- Achieving goals through servant leadership and teamwork.

- Commitment to high standards and the pursuit of excellence.

- Accountability as a means to elevate individual and corporate performance.

- Innovation as a fundamental driver of long-term success.

- Embracing change as an opportunity to learn and improve.

- Contributing to the communities where we live and work.

- Perseverance through an abiding faith and optimism.

Once these values were established, we focused on how to incorporate them into the culture and gain employee commitment. The goal was for employees to rely upon and reflect these principles in their daily actions and interactions with each other, our clients, prospects, vendors, and stakeholders. Today, each member of our management team is committed to communicating and demonstrating these values on a daily basis. We know that it is important to lead by example, which is consistent with our servant leadership style of management that I will discuss in chapter ten.

Long-Term Commitment

Formulating a culture is not a "one and done" task; it's something that you implement over the long haul, taking concrete actions to make it into something real. Practice what you preach, in other words.

Unfortunately, this is where most companies fall short. Creating a mission statement and set of values alone will not help a company build the culture it seeks; rather, an ongoing series of actions and programs, supported by a strong commitment at the top level, bring a culture into being.

Most companies simply post their mission and values statements in the front entrance or break room and never give them a second thought. Done this way, the mission and values aren't actually reinforced and internalized. They should become part of the company's very DNA. Otherwise, organizations with neglected cultures or unclear direction suffer from low employee morale and crippled productivity, and often find it difficult to align the interests of its employees with the firm's important objectives. And yet the leaders wonder why so many culture initiatives fail to thrive.

"Show the Culture": Actions Speak Louder than Words

We've been able to "institutionalize" the culture we designed for Insperity by creating programs that support the core values. All of our employee programs, from the new-employee orientation to the annual climate survey, are patterned after those values that undergird our culture and our human capital strategy in general.

I like to call this "showing the culture"—concrete, visible proof that we're living out our values. Here are a few examples from our organization that may provide a framework for your company.

Integrity

Early on, integrity was one of the most important characteristics we sought in employees. We define integrity as "doing what you say you are going to do," which reflects our faith-based personal morals and is something we wanted to ingrain in the daily habits of our personnel. After all, our client relationships were based on trust; the business owners we serve lean on us to help them succeed. This held us to a higher standard of accountability and responsibility to each other, our clients, and our shareholders. Integrity was—and always has been—the foundation of Insperity's corporate culture.

The funny thing about integrity (or lack thereof) is that it manifests in ways big and small. We strive to demonstrate integrity at the highest levels, whether in the face of a major crisis (as I'll talk about in chapter ten) or in ordinary day-to-day interactions with each other and with employees.

As a CEO, your integrity is going to be tested; you might even be tempted to take the selfish route instead of the principled one when faced with a problem. Don't. Your word is everything. Take it from us.

Work-Life Balance

Another important aspect of our culture is a work-life balance. From the beginning, we sought to create an organization where people work to live, not live to work. *Everyone* benefits when employees find a healthy equilibrium between their professional and personal lives, because this sharpens their focus and intensifies their engagement at work, enabling them to better serve our client companies.

Insperity has institutionalized this aspect of our culture in several ways. We give full-time employees paid time off (PTO) that is accrued based on their length of tenure. This encourages them to step away from the office and enjoy life outside of the office. And when they return, they're recharged and focused.

Although we don't formally have a flexible working program, supervisors have the discretion to allow flexibility when it's appropriate, which is beneficial to the organization and employees alike. Whether it's allowing an employee to work at home for a period of time or providing a flexible schedule for employees who travel farther distances to avoid heavy traffic, we accommodate the needs of our people. Flexibility is essential to driving a productive culture, and allowing employees this option has yielded great results.

A Caring Philosophy

Many employees have described how working at Insperity is like working with family. Our people have always had a natural tendency to rally together and support each other during difficult times, especially when an employee is dealing with an unforeseen personal tragedy. Often, our team members have organized voluntary collections or provided meals to their coworkers going through a time of need. Over the years, we came to realize that many employees who are faced with an unexpected financial crisis often did not have a place to turn to for help. When our employees hear about a coworker enduring a catastrophic event, they often ask how they can lend a hand.

We've channeled this altruistic spirit into the development of some great programs. For example, a hardship-compensation program helps qualified employees who need to take time away from work due to an injury or illness, or to care for a family member, to apply for a maximum number of paid compensation days (in addition to short-term disability when applicable). This PTO bank is supported by employees who donate any remaining PTO hours at the end of each year.

Additionally, we have an employee-benevolence program that is anonymously funded by employees, for employees. Confidentially managed by a third-party organization, employees who need emergency financial assistance can draw on the support of The Insperity Fund, which is subsidized by the generosity of other Insperity employees. This program has raised more than $3.3 million, which have helped nearly four hundred people pay for necessities such as utilities, mortgages, and car repairs. The fund has been a godsend for those who needed it, and for those who have supported it, a way of reaching out and reinforcing valued personal connections with their fellow workers.

In the same vein, we actively encourage our people to give back to their communities. After all, our mission is "Helping businesses succeed so communities prosper." Our Caring Employees program allots each employee up to twelve paid hours every quarter to participate in company-sponsored events or personal volunteer opportunities. Additionally, volunteerism has served as a powerful team-building activity, which supports our core value of "achieving goals through servant leadership and teamwork." This is an example of how a positive, well-designed corporate culture can be self-reinforcing: if you choose your values well, they'll feed off and strengthen each other.

The program has expanded to include matching gifts and a volunteer-recognition program that honors two employees quarterly and annually for their community service. The annual award winners receive an individual gift and a grant toward the charity of their choice.

One recent initiative that made me proud to lead such a community-minded company was our involvement in the Hurricane Harvey relief effort. In collaboration with other organizations, Insperity established the Lake Houston Area Relief Fund (LHARF) to aid families and businesses impacted by the disaster. The LHARF was modeled after Insperity's own internal initiatives—a testament to those initiatives' success.

We donated $1 million to The Insperity Fund to support the sixty-five corporate families displaced by the hurricane. We also donated another $1 million to LHARF as a matching grant to encourage others to donate as well. The catastrophe affected countless people in Texas and beyond, including our own customers and employees, and recovery demanded that all of us work together. The most impressive response to the natural disaster was the way employees performed rescue and recovery, immediate support and clean-up, as well as how they continued to follow through in the long rebuilding process. Our people demonstrated our culture in a powerful way in a time of need.

Our philanthropic efforts also extend toward assisting our nonprofit client companies. Not only are our employees encouraged to volunteer their time with these client companies, but we set aside some discretionary spending that goes toward supporting those nonprofits. Remaining funds in the volunteer budget at the end of the year are automatically rolled into an annual grant fund, to which client companies can apply for support of the charitable causes of their choice.

Philanthropy is its own reward, but it's good for business, too—in particular, for the brand. Today, Insperity is widely recognized for its giving spirit. As one woman with whom we volunteered said, "Whenever there is something good happening in our community, if you dig deep enough, you will find Insperity behind it."

Employee Recognition

An employee recognition program can serve as a powerful motivator by formally acknowledging employees for their hard work. It's a worthwhile investment in your human capital strategy because it communicates to your whole workforce which behaviors are promoted on a consistent basis. We reward employees who model certain company values: excellence, commitment, service, teamwork, and productivity. Publicly acknowledging their contributions helps to ensure these key attributes are ingrained into our culture. And it's not just a top-down system of rewards bestowed by the higher-ups: a peer recognition system allows coworkers to nominate each other for the award, signaling that the values that make up our culture are not just words on a poster—they're personal attributes that we practice daily. Plus, employees have to know the values and behaviors we reward well enough to recognize them in others to nominate their coworkers. That's what institutionalizing the culture really means.

Employee Surveys: Taking the Organization's Temperature

As an HR company, we're held to a higher standard when it comes to our own corporate culture. How can we help other companies improve upon their culture if we can't get it right ourselves?

One way we make sure we're staying on track is through employee surveys that gauge how our people feel at work and how well they think we're upholding our own values. The surveys include questions such as, "Do you have the resources and tools to perform your job? Is your opinion valued? Are you satisfied in your job? Do you feel like your manager listens to you?" These kinds of questions serve as a barometer of the emotional health of the business.

Historically, we have used the Gallup Q12 Employee Engagement Survey to benchmark against the best places to work throughout the world. Gallup's employee engagement work is based on more than thirty years of in-depth behavioral economic research involving more than thirty-five million employees. Through rigorous research, Gallup has identified twelve core elements—the Q12—that link powerfully to key business outcomes. The twelve questions from the Gallup engagement model are interspersed within our survey and the results are compared to the average and to "World Class" status determined by Gallup. The survey categorizes the respondents into three categories, "engaged," "not engaged," and maybe most importantly, "actively disengaged." The goal is to have all employees rowing in sync in the same direction, but the reality is all organizations have a percentage of employees that are not just passive, but are actually creating a drag on others and the company. We depict the outcome using the graphic below and report back to employees along with the rest of the results. As you can see, Insperity scores well against the average and is comfortably above the "World Class" level with 82 percent engaged and 18 percent not engaged or actively disengaged compared to 70 percent and 30 percent respectively against the benchmark.

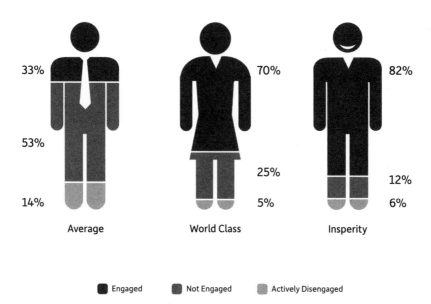

The picture isn't always so rosy. For example, a few years ago, our rewards and compensation area experienced a dip in ratings. In response, we made adjustments to enhance certain programs. This, by the way, is key—if you conduct surveys, make sure you take action in response. Otherwise, people might dismiss the whole thing as a mere administrative exercise.

Another common sticking point for employees is promotions— how they're decided and who gets them. Our surveys have been used to inform our approach to this area too. All in all, the survey results provide a source of valuable feedback that let us know what's working, and what we need to make better.

Be sure to consider not just the responses themselves, but the participation rate. How many employees participate in the survey can also reflect an organization's "cultural health." If there is a lot of distrust in your organization, the participation rate among employees is going to be pretty low. That's a red flag.

As I said, one of the best ways to evaluate your company's culture is to simply ask the employees, "What's it like to work here?" Listen to their answers, adapt, make changes, and ask again.

The problem with being the person on top is, well, you're on top. And sometimes the distance between the tip of the pyramid and the bottom can be very long. Even the most empathetic, ear-to-the-ground CEOs are prone to losing a bit of perspective from where they're perched. Employee surveys keep you connected with the people you care about.

Four Easy Steps to Creating a Great Culture

I get it: culture is one of those tasks that is easier said than done. Most business leaders grasp the concept of corporate culture, and they understand why it's valuable, but actually *creating* it and implementing it (making it an active part of employees' day-to-day work life) is another story. Even though Jerry and I had a clear vision for the kind of place we wanted to build, it took a lot of trial and error to make it happen.

So, let's lay it out in a more methodical way. The following is a simple four-point plan to guide you—the same plan that we used to build a culture that our employees love.

Step One: Lay a foundation

Creating a company culture doesn't happen overnight. It's a process—one that starts with establishing your mission, vision, and values. You and your executive team need to devote time and effort to determine these company cornerstones. If you don't, someone will fill in the gap. And one day, you'll wake up, look around and say, "This wasn't what we set out to create. What happened?"

Discuss with your executive team the values you all hold dear. What drives you? What are you passionate about? These are your values, and this is where company culture lives.

Step Two: Take the temperature

Culture depends on employee engagement (and vice versa). Disengaged employees can be a drain on money, productivity, and morale. A culture survey (also known as a climate survey) is a great way of learning what employees think and feel about their job, workplace, colleagues, and managers.

Trust is key in company culture—if your people don't trust you, they're not going to follow you. An employee survey is a method of building that trust, because it communicates that you care about their feelings, needs, and wants. If it helps, use a third party to conduct the survey and make it anonymous for your employees.

Finally, commit to acting on the survey results. Your employees will doubt your sincerity if no changes come out of the results. Use the information to find new ways of ensuring the current climate aligns with the company culture and its core values.

Step Three: Get buy-ins

Before you finalize any culture development plan, solicit your employees' input. After all, they're the ones who will be most affected by it, day in and day out.

A focus group involving employees from different departments, experience levels, and job titles is helpful. It is not necessary to include supervisors, managers, or executives; just the employees. Employee feedback can be eye-opening. What you thought would be an insignificant matter may be a point of great concern for employees, and what they describe as compelling may not have registered high on your meter.

In the end, it's your company, your vision, your values. But if you've hired people you trust, then it's worth hearing what they have to say.

Then, along with your executive team, review the feedback and make tweaks as you see fit. Once you have the final version, you need to secure buy-ins from your management team as well. They, too, must live these values every day at work. Everyone must walk the walk.

Step Four: Roll it out

Embedding the culture in the fabric of the organization requires more than just putting it on a break room poster. Your company culture is a living element. It impacts all aspects of the organization: From the way you handle performance reviews to how you recognize outstanding employees for their contribution, it all connects to your human-resources infrastructure. It will reflect on how you hire, onboard, and fire. It impacts everything.

If what you crave is a strategic atmosphere with a competitive edge for talent, then shape the culture accordingly. Make it so that people will want to work for you, to build long-term careers with you. Your culture must be strong enough to entice them, and strong enough to keep them. And many companies fall short. Don't be one of them.

Thinking Strategically:

1. Your corporate culture is your organization's unique personality. Another way of looking at it is this: If your employees were asked, "What is it like to work at your company?" how would they respond? Would their responses reflect your company's mission and values?

2. The link between company culture and employee personality is a two-way street: the culture influences your people's attitudes and behaviors, and the employees' own personalities are reflected in and shape the culture. Consider what personal characteristics you would you like to see in employees; let that guide how you wish to shape the environment of the organization.

Thinking Systematically:

1. Culture doesn't really mean anything if it's not practiced in visible and concrete ways. Implement programs that allow the core values to be realized on a daily basis.

2.   Devise a means of measuring your progress toward achieving the culture you desire. Annual employee surveys are useful for this purpose. Just make sure you act on the results.

3.   Creating a corporate culture is not just issuing an edict from on high, even if it's designed by the executive team. You should solicit the input of the workforce, and you should strive to achieve buy-ins from all levels of the organization. Only then does the culture become a vibrant part of the company's anatomy.

CHAPTER FOUR

Strategy #2: Finding, Hiring, and Keeping the Best

RECRUITING, SELECTION, AND RETENTION

Many business leaders don't realize that many of the problems they encounter are the result of a flaw in their HR practices—and, in particular, their recruiting and selection strategy.

During Insperity's early years, I often accompanied our staff on sales calls. During one particularly stressful sales pitch, the sales associate opened the dialogue with the business owner by asking, "What are your HR problems?"

The business owner replied, "I don't have any HR problems."

Of course, upon hearing this, I couldn't restrain myself, so I had to interject. "You know, we're not just interested in your HR issues," I said. "What are the biggest issues you have to deal with in your business in general?"

The business owner replied, "My problem is sales."

"*Really?*" I said. I knew this was my chance. "So, let me ask you—how many sales people do you have?"

The business owner said the company had about a dozen sales employees.

I then replied, "Out of those twelve sales people, do you have two or three who are really knocking it out of the park? And do you have six to eight who are pretty good, but who are hit-or-miss? And then do you have a few that are not really accomplishing a lot, and if you really thought about it, you might be wondering why they're still around?"

He looked at me like I had read his mind.

"What if we administered a personality-profiling tool and had your staff complete it?" I asked. "And what if we could alter your recruiting process so that the next two or three people you hire are more like the two or three top performers? And if you had two or three ready to hire who could perform at that level, wouldn't you want to replace those few that are hanging at the bottom?"

Although the business owner had said he had a sales problem, what he really had was an HR problem, or at least there was an HR solution to his sales problem. This is a frequent scenario, where business leaders neglect the importance of consistently hiring the types of employees that best fit the organization. In our company, we have a very specific sales profile that we recruit against, which is critical to ensuring that we continuously hire the right people for our sales organization.

Big-League Recruiting Strategies

Professional football teams expend a staggering amount of effort to evaluate potential talent. Prospective athletes endure a rigorous and extensive process that includes skills tests, interviews, exams, and extensive background checks. But other factors—such as the team's culture—also play an important role in the selection of a player. Many times, a trade or draft pick is made based on how well the potential player will "fit in their system." Each team has a system—the unique way they want to play the game that they believe will position them to win. It may emphasize speed over strength or running over passing. Regardless, their player-selection strategy is intricately linked to this system.

The rigor of this selection process is something entrepreneurs should mimic in their own recruiting, selection, and retention efforts. The recruiting process should start with a strategic plan that includes key traits and attributes you would like to see in your employees in general. There should also be well-defined job descriptions and a systematic process for screening, interviewing, and selecting the right people for the right positions. Next, a new-hire process should be mapped out to help acclimate them to the company's culture and expectations. And most important, there must be an ongoing support system to ensure your people—the organization's most valuable assets—are actively engaged in their role in order to avoid losing them.

Most organizations actually don't have a recruiting strategy or hiring philosophy. They just haphazardly wing it. But this is not something that is simply going to "fall in place." Many business leaders view the hiring process as a necessary evil rather than as an opportunity—a position is vacant, and the company needs to fill it quickly. But this myopic approach is fraught with risk.

When the wrong person is hired, everyone in the organization suffers. Companies can lose thousands of dollars, especially when the average cost of replacing an employee ranges from 75 to 150 percent of the employee's salary. Not to mention the financial and emotional drain caused by a lawsuit or employment claim filed by a disgruntled employee. The countless hours of lost productivity and lowered employee morale also take a toll on the organization. And the loss of intellectual capital that walks out the door is immeasurable. The bottom line: businesses cannot afford bad hires, nor can they afford to lose good people.

Strategic Preparation Prevents Costly Mistakes

Here's a common recruiting scenario: a client company is scrambling to hire several hundred employees after winning a large contract. Unfortunately, without a recruiting plan in place, the company isn't prepared to meet the high-volume recruiting that the new business requires. They may be able to find enough warm bodies to fill the chairs, but the likelihood of finding the right talent is low, and the odds of a hiring mistake are high. As a result, they struggle to capitalize on the growth opportunity afforded by the big contract, and in the scramble to put the right people in place, they commit costly errors that afflict the firm for months or even years.

We've seen client companies go through this situation many times, so when it happened again recently to one firm, we knew what to do. Fortunately, we were able to streamline their manual process and design a recruiting plan that fit their needs. By establishing and implementing the right processes, we helped the client company interview, screen, and verify certifications of more than a thousand applicants so they could bring on the most qualified employees—ones who fit the organization's culture—in three months.

Like flood insurance, or jumper cables, a strong recruiting strategy is something you want to have *ahead* of time, not when you suddenly find you need it. This is one of the keys of successful recruiting, selection, and retention: advance planning. This may prove to be challenging, but it's the most effective way to conduct a successful talent search and minimize costly hiring mistakes.

There are also those business leaders who are at the opposite end of the spectrum—they overextend and unintentionally invest too many resources into their recruiting efforts. And unfortunately, this can backfire.

For example, a client company with about 500 employees wanted to expand its sales operation. Unfortunately, the company was suffering from a 50 percent employee turnover rate, and its recruiting costs were averaging more than $1.5 million annually. After assessing the client's recruiting and retention process, Insperity's recruiting specialists worked closely with the client to develop an effective employment-branding campaign, which incorporated a message tailored specifically to the type of applicants the company was targeting. Additionally, Insperity worked with the organization's leaders to implement behavioral-based interviewing and selection training, which included preparing hiring managers to better evaluate the competencies of candidates to ensure they matched the demands of the position and the needs of the company generally. The client company also added pre-employment assessments and background checks to further maximize recruiting efforts and dollars.

As a result, the client company's employee turnover rate decreased by more than 30 percent, and the organization's recruiting costs were trimmed by more than $1 million. A well-thought-out recruiting strategy is a major cost and time saver.

The president of a software development company in Atlanta could tell you a thing or two about recruiting. For five years, a client had been working with Insperity to assist with health benefits and payroll, before enrolling in the full spectrum of services, which included recruiting.

As the president tells it, Insperity was an immense boon to the company's recruiting efforts, helping to replace 50 percent of their staff within twelve months. "That can be so disruptive to a small company, but we did a lot of this intentionally with Insperity's help and improved the quality of our personnel," says the owner. "Put me up against any company our size with the same resources, and on any given day I can out-recruit and out-train that company, because I have Insperity … We're able to fill voids and expand our company in a timely manner that we couldn't accomplish otherwise."

Hiring Strategies

Finding the Right Fit

The previous chapter discussed the primacy of the organization's culture as the cornerstone of a human capital strategy. The culture touches all aspects of the organization, and the recruiting and selection process is no exception. An applicant's skills and experience are obviously important, but to what extent the candidate's own personality will fit in the organization's unique environment should be given equal consideration.

This means having a clear sense of the attributes, characteristics, and work habits the organization values most in its employees. For example, a highly competitive environment that encourages individual performance may require a different recruiting plan than an organization that prioritizes teamwork and collaboration. An individual's qualifications for an open position is determined as much by individual talent as by his or her impact on the team and the organization of which he or she will form a part.

Throughout Insperity's history, we've seen several examples of new hires who had the requisite skills and experience, but a poor cultural fit made their employment unviable. Sometimes a very strong individual performer had a detrimental effect on others, and the working team suffered as a whole. These are difficult situations, because the individual may have excellent personal performance metrics, but leaves a wake behind that slows the progress of others. A good cultural fit ensures a positive effect on fellow employees.

I recall another cautionary tale that happened with a client company whose business was closely tied to a particular sport. A departing employee, who had the right skills and performed well in the position, had no interest in the sport. Though he performed his job competently, the lack of passion came through loud and clear to customers and fellow employees. So, when it came time to find his replacement, our recruiting specialists made every effort to communicate clearly and whittle down the applicant pool to those who had the required skills *and* possessed a demonstrated interest in the sport that was so important to the organization's business.

Recruiting candidates whose attributes closely reflect your organization's culture improve the odds for hiring the best one. We look beyond the basic skills, education, and experience required for the role. We consider individuals who value integrity, exhibit a positive attitude, maintain a high energy level, possess a good sense of humor, and most importantly, demonstrate a caring or customer-centric personality. This serves to attract someone who would uphold and feel energized by Insperity's values and beliefs.

Attraction goes both ways. While you're looking for candidates who are a good fit, prospective employees are also searching for companies whose culture will resonate with *them*. Remember that job candidates aren't just looking for a job—they're looking for a brand experience. Where they work becomes a part of their identity and a reflection on them personally. Use your unique corporate brand as a selling point to attract top talent. I know that it might seem tempting to put this cultural stuff on the back burner, especially if you're a young company struggling to get off the ground. "I gotta find someone with a sense of humor?" you might think. "It's hard enough just to fill the role with someone who can perform well and show up on time!" "Culture-congruent" recruiting is not just for the big players; in fact, in a smaller company, one could even argue that it's more important. Because you might not yet be established, you might be in the red, you might even be in sink-or-swim mode. But if you pick your people right, your culture will always provide firm footing, no matter what is happening with the bottom line. And that's a powerful thing.

Job Descriptions

One of the most important (and most overlooked) components of the recruiting process is developing and maintaining written job descriptions. Many companies *think* they have formalized, written job descriptions on hand, but in our experience, we've found this is not the case. In fact, among our client companies, 71 percent of clients reported using job descriptions, but our own analysis showed that only 20 percent of the jobs within those organizations had actual written descriptions.

Hiring without a job description is like going grocery shopping without a list. But with the right planning, your chances of getting exactly what you need are higher, and you cut down on wasteful meandering around the aisles.

Moreover, maintaining accurate written descriptions of each position is not just an administrative formality: clear job descriptions protect employers against potential lawsuits, in addition to their main purpose of ensuring the right person is hired for the job.

Even when job descriptions do exist, they're often inadequate—they're too vague and fail to articulate the details and expectations of the position. This impedes the recruiting process for obvious reasons, but its negative impact can extend well beyond the job interview, affecting the first few weeks or months of a new hire's tenure, when they show up and—surprise!—the job they have is a little different from the one they thought they were hired for.

Explicitly outlining the expectations and responsibilities from the get-go establishes a clear set of standards for new employees to internalize during the recruiting and onboarding process. They know exactly what to expect—and what's expected of them—from the first moment they sit down at their desks.

This all seems intuitive, but you'd be surprised at how many organizations fail to adhere to this simple practice, causing unnecessary confusion from the very start of an employee's tenure. Needless to say, it's a bad way to begin a working relationship.

At Insperity, we provide employees with a copy of their official job description, and we require they sign it to avoid ambiguity and to minimize employer liability (a topic I'll delve into further in chapter six). Employers should also update job descriptions periodically, perhaps in conjunction with an annual review cycle, and especially when any of the functions and/or requirements change.

Hiring Manager Training

Creating a durable framework through which your hiring managers make their decisions is key to consistently finding top people who fit your company. This framework should be strategic and systematic: strategic in that it accords with a long-term vision for the company, and systematic in that it is carried out according to a standardized set of rules and processes which everyone adheres to.

First, an effective recruiting program requires consistent decision-making across the organization. That means training hiring managers accordingly, so they're all on the same page. A clear recruiting protocol is necessary for choosing the right candidate. For example, you're a hiring manager who has to select between three very qualified people. Even when they're similarly qualified, distinguishing among them can feel like making an apples-to-oranges comparison. Each brings a unique set of experiences and personality traits; each has his or her particular pros and cons. Who to choose?

Well, if you have gone through the process in a consistent fashion, you can compare them more easily. You can examine their answers to the standardized questions you've asked of all of them, allowing you to make a clear, side-by-side assessment as to who the best fit is.

Consistency streamlines and strengthens the hiring process. Our corporate recruiters work closely with hiring managers to ensure both teams are looking for the same competencies. Recruiters are the custodians of the process. They're constantly looking for good people to refer to the hiring managers, who might hire only two or three people each year (especially in a competitive labor market). Both positions are essential for attracting top talent, and if they're operating from the same playbook, it makes the whole process easier, more fluid, and more successful.

Behavioral-based interviewing is a critical element in our corporate and client company recruiting efforts. This interview strategy involves asking candidates how they might handle certain hypothetical scenarios or even real-life situations they've encountered in the past. The technique is often more revelatory than the standard "where do you see yourself in five years?" interview questions and furnishes the recruiter with more nuanced insight into the mind and behavior of the candidate. The hiring manager should be trained to look for key attributes, behaviors, skills, and knowledge that can help determine whether the applicant is qualified for the position and fits the culture.

Additionally, laying the groundwork and establishing ethical and legal guidelines for hiring managers to follow during the recruiting and selection process minimizes potential employer-liability issues. For example, hiring managers should have a thorough understanding of which questions are appropriate (and legal) to ask during the interview process, and which ones should be avoided.

Advertising and Marketing

Recruiting is similar to sales: you're selling your organization to a potential candidate just as you would a customer. The company is the product, and the environment, location, and other benefits are the perks that come with it. Apply the same strategic acumen to recruiting that you use when marketing to prospective clients.

It's important to develop an "employment brand," which should be tied to the company's culture and communicate the advantages that the organization offers its employees. This brand is the reason why employees join an organization and why they stay. The marketplace is saturated with big and small organizations that are all competing to attract the best candidates. Your organization's recruitment messaging must be honest, consistent, and congruent with the attitude and spirit of the company in order to best your competitors. The message should target the types of individuals you want to "buy" your company. Tout its best attributes; confidently convey what makes you unique in your industry. Ideally, you want potential hires to contact *you* for a job. That's when you know you're doing something right.

Many businesses fail to market and advertise a position accurately, or they communicate an inaccurate impression of the working environment there. Believe me, you're not doing yourself any favors by misleading people about your workplace environment. For example, a client wanted us to paint a "picture-perfect" image of the company to entice prospective candidates. Consequently, a lot of people eagerly applied. But after candidates met with the employer, they quickly lost interest in the job. In turns out that this business owner was tough and demanding (a quality that was readily apparent during the interviews), which was a far cry from how the company had portrayed itself in the job postings.

As a result, Insperity's recruiting specialists recommended the company take a more candid and straightforward approach in marketing the position and suggested they describe the business owner's management style upfront. This strategy paid off for the client, which was then able to recruit the right type of candidates— the kind of people who not only didn't mind working for that kind of employer, but actually thrived in a high-pressure atmosphere.

It's really all about attracting the right people for the right job, and that also means targeting your budget where it will have maximal impact. Place ads strategically. Consider media in local and surrounding markets that can generate a flow of *qualified* applicants. Obviously, the internet has revolutionized recruiting, especially given social media's influence on employment-branding initiatives. As a result, Insperity's recruiting services have shifted its advertising and marketing focus to building and engaging online communities around the Insperity brand and employment culture on the major social-media channels, including LinkedIn, Twitter, and Facebook. We also encourage our corporate employees to participate in social media to showcase their own professional expertise and further market Insperity as an employer of choice. In a healthy organization, the CEO is not the only public face of the company. Everyone, from top to bottom, represents the company and its brand. If you hire strategically, you can be confident in your organization's public image.

Employer brand is a term commonly used to describe a company's reputation as an organization and employer. The brand is determined by the experiences of current and former employees, applicants, candidates, and those with a professional interest in the organization. It's what the public remembers when they think about the company.

An employer brand exists whether or not it was designed through a formal process. The key is to harness the power behind the brand to create a positive message to candidates.

Candidate behavior is evolving into a career consumer mind-set. This career consumer mind-set has led to an increase in online review platforms that help to lift the veil of what it is like to work at a particular organization, while allowing potential employees to make a more informed decision about their future careers.

Today, candidates do their research and often access numerous data points like a company's website, LinkedIn page, search engine results, and online review platforms like Glassdoor before ever deciding to submit their application to a company. These same platforms also allow current and past employees to weigh in on their experience working at an organization, helping to create the message that new candidates receive.

How influential are these employer review sites? In a recent poll by SoftwareAdvice.com, job seekers were asked how Glassdoor affected their application decisions when looking for new roles. They found that almost half of job seekers read Glassdoor reviews before ever deciding to apply for jobs. In addition, 25 percent of job seekers did not apply to jobs after reading negative reviews of compensation and benefits.

A brand's reputation already exists on a number of sites such as Google, Glassdoor and Indeed because of candidate and employee feedback. As an organization, it is imperative to be a part of the already ongoing conversation.

Here are some things to consider:

- Does the company already have any reviews on Google or Glassdoor?

- Is the overall feedback positive or negative?

- Are there any responses to positive or negative reviews?

- Is the company's contact information available?

- Are there any pictures of the company?

- Are the responses to the negative reviews polite and respectful?

- Is the page updated, and does it show frequent engagement?

Being seen as a part of the conversation through responses and updated content helps employers maintain a say in their employment brand and the messaging surrounding their organization.

Regardless of the latest trends, it's still important to be selective with your online recruiting. Don't just throw everything at the wall and see what sticks—a tempting prospect sometimes, given the dizzying array of options when it comes to online marketing. Instead, target your resources where they'll generate the most results. We've found numerous qualified candidates for our client companies using a proprietary online recruiting tool that allows us to conveniently and cost-effectively attract potential applicants. We use it in our own recruiting as well.

In spite of the "technologization" of recruiting, the old-fashioned ways still have clout. Leverage the speed and convenience of Skype interviews when it suits you, but don't forget that nothing beats a face-to-face interview when it comes to getting a feel for a person's character and how he or she will engage with customers and colleagues.

Recruiting Internally

Companies should also consider recruiting for positions internally, which can be a cost-effective means of finding the right person. Posting job openings internally not only allows the company to address its personnel needs, it provides valuable growth opportunities for employees.

In addition, your own employees serve as great recruiters for external candidates. Like attracts like, so an employee who is happy and productive within the organization will probably know others who would also be a good fit. Word-of-mouth recruitment is a big part of Insperity—our people know what we look for in a potential recruit and they can provide first-hand knowledge and information about our organization to their contacts. As an incentive, many companies pay a bonus for employee referrals who become new hires.

The Case for Background Checks

The frequency with which business owners skip this important step in the selection process is astounding. But pre-employment screening and testing is a *necessity*, not an option, when it comes to selecting the right employees. Drug testing, personality assessments, skills tests, and background checks help pinpoint whether the person is the right fit for the company. And these measures also reduce potential employer liabilities. Unfortunately, many businesses endure the high price and harmful effects of hiring without administering a professional background check, which reveals any potential problems with a candidate *before* an offer is extended and prevents costly headaches down the road.

It's also important to understand that not all background checks are equal. There's a significant difference between the services provided by a professional screening company and those of an online, instant-check service. An online service typically relies on porous and outdated data and may not abide by the consumer protections mandated by the Fair Credit Reporting Act (FCRA) and other applicable laws.

Professional-screening firms, in contrast, go directly to the source repositories that maintain records to provide more comprehensive and accurate data and faster results. They also protect their clients by adhering to the ever-changing bevy of national, state, and local laws.

Missing out on hiring the best candidates because of slow or sloppy background checks, or making a bad hiring decision based on faulty information in a person's report, can be financially costly, especially for a small business. Take it from our many years of experience in this area—tread carefully.

How to Woo Candidates You Can't Afford

In any industry, the best professionals know their worth. And especially if you're an SMB, you might find that an excellent candidate for a position is worth (or demands) more than what you can afford. It's a tough scenario, because money talks, and if you can't match their salary demands, they might walk. However, in your favor is the fact that the top performers don't always simply gravitate to the highest bidder. You can entice them with non-monetary perks.

For one, the culture itself can be a big draw. Excellent employees want to work in a positive, forward-thinking environment where their intellect is respected, their creativity is encouraged, and their emotional needs are met. Also, don't forget, smaller organizations have an advantage over big companies. Emphasize the opportunity for employees to really make a difference and see the direct result of their efforts. Some senior professionals might be at a point in their career where they're less excited by money than by authority, influence, and the desire for a less-political work environment than that of the larger corporation. In addition, tout your company's benefits, especially if the package is generous or offers unusual perks that your competitors might lack (such as flexible work schedules).

One word of caution as you negotiate with a desirable candidate who is sitting on the fence: try to figure out what's important to that individual. If it's obvious that his or her top priority is a high salary, then even if you manage to persuade the candidate to sign on, you might just end up losing him or her a year or two later to a company that *can* pay the high-dollar figure. It can be tough to let a good person go, but sometimes, it's just not the right fit.

Onboarding New Employees

Half of all hourly workers leave within in the first four months of being hired, and half of senior outside hires depart within eighteen months, according to a 2010 report by Talya Bauer of the SHRM Foundation.[2] The worst scenario for new employees is to start at a new position and not have a clear idea of what is expected of them, or even to doubt whether they belong there at all. Obviously, getting off on the wrong foot is bad for both the new hire and the team to which he or she belongs; in the worst case, it might mean losing the employee just days after his or her start date.

Employers must develop and maintain an onboarding process that not only teaches employees about the company's culture and general corporate expectations, but also clearly defines the specific guidelines and processes of the position. Our client companies benefit greatly when, with our assistance, they implement a new-hire orientation process, which shortens the learning curve and speeds past the (let's face it) tedious first-week administrative tasks so that the employee can become a contributing member of the organization quickly.

Ideally, the onboarding process should start as soon as possible after a job offer is accepted—no need to wait until the first day of work. Recognize that onboarding goes beyond the basic orientation and first-day meet-and-greets to include the entire strategic process of helping new employees get integrated.

Bauer posits that a standard onboarding regimen should consist of four parts:

---

2   Talya N. Bauer, "Onboarding New Employees: Maximizing Success," SHRM Foundation's Effective Practice Guidelines Series, 2010, https://www.shrm.org/foundation/ourwork/initiatives/resources-from-past-initiatives/Documents/Onboarding%20New%20Employees.pdf.

1. **Compliance**: Familiarizing employees with the applicable rules and regulations.

2. **Clarification**: Making sure the new employees comprehend their role and the organization's expectations.

3. **Culture:** Familiarizing the employee with the norms and general environment of the company.

4. **Connection**: Starting the process (which will continue for the duration of the employee's tenure at the firm) of building interpersonal relationships and professional connections between the new hire and his or her colleagues.[3]

Finally, don't forget that onboarding should also be *strategic* in nature—cover the essential administrative nuts and bolts, but always be thinking of the organization's broader vision and mission. The onboarding process should teach them about the business model and make clear the connections between company-wide goals and their day-to-day tasks.

Retention: Keeping Top Performers

Considering the sizable investment of time, energy, and funds involved in recruiting, and given the scarcity and value of outstanding people, businesses have an acute need to retain their best employees. Don't get complacent here—even if your most proficient people are thriving in their roles and are generally content with their positions, they can still be tempted by outside offers. After all, your competitors also have a need for skilled workers—and they won't hesitate to poach your people if they can.

---

3   Ibid.

Retention is not just a matter of salary. Sometimes employees are lured by the prospect of a pay boost at a different firm, but some of the most frequently cited reasons for top performers moving on relate to issues with the employee's direct supervisor, management in general, or the culture of the company. Hence, the source of dissatisfaction also lies at the emotional level—with the need to feel appreciated for making a valuable contribution. Bear this in mind as you develop a retention strategy to keep your top performers—salary is a factor, but emotional well-being is of equal importance.

Examples of proven retention strategies include:

- **Reward and recognition**. Motivate employees to perform well in their jobs and feel good about their contributions to the organization by obtaining recognition from their peers and management. This can be as simple as monthly recognition in an employee newsletter or a monthly, quarterly, and annual awards program. We're big on recognizing individual achievement at Insperity. Chapter five, on compensation, recognition, and reward strategy, explores this critical area further.

- **Training and development**. Encourage and provide opportunities for employees to acquire new skills and develop both intellectually and professionally. Working closely with employees to determine their short- and long-term goals permits them to cultivate careers, not just jobs, and helps ensure that they stay challenged and fulfilled at work. I will also discuss this in greater detail in chapter ten.

- **Communication and feedback**. Provide employees and management with opportunities for two-way communication to head off any potential problems. This keeps the door open and shows employees that their feelings and feedback are valued. Be sincere and specific. Leaders should be trained to demonstrate appreciation on an informal, day-to-day basis, and not just during the annual awards ceremony (though ceremonies and big corporate events are important, too). Letting employees know you value their commitment, dedication, talent, and performance can go a *long* way. Never underestimate the power of a simple, well-deserved compliment. I'll share more communication wisdom in chapter eleven.

Exit Interviews

When an employee leaves your organization, take the time to conduct an exit interview to find out why. Typically, valuable employees don't look for other job opportunities if they're being treated well by an organization that appreciates them.

When our company was smaller and its workforce more geographically concentrated, we had the luxury of speaking face-to-face with employees before they left. And as the company expanded, maintaining this personal interaction was important. Some employees prefer to submit their feedback to us via a form rather than an in-person chat, but regardless of the communication method, we always value their input, and they value the chance to speak frankly about the positive and negative aspects of their experience. Regardless of the employee's status with the company upon leaving, this system serves to provide each employee with closure to move on and provides the employer with valuable information to improve further.

When an employee gives critical feedback, our corporate HR staff reviews it and assesses the situation with that employee's supervisor. Each quarter, general managers receive an "at-a-glance" summary to evaluate the exit interview data, which serves to uncover any areas that may need further investigation. We've also revised the exit interview questions by aligning them with our culture survey to find out if there are any gaps between the company's culture and its practices.

There's no one right way to conduct exit interviews, but in our experience with client companies, a few basic guidelines are advisable. Following these steps go a long way to ensuring a productive, mutually satisfying process.

First, give the employee some advance notice of what will be talked about. There's no reason to keep the interview questions shrouded in secrecy. When you start the meeting, clearly state your objectives, and assure the employee no adverse consequences will result, even if their answers are critical or they feel the need to vent. This is their time to speak freely—again, allowing them this freedom is beneficial for both them and for the organization. Ask open-ended questions, and let the interviewee do most of the talking.

Thinking Strategically:

1. A big part of recruiting involves "selling" your company to prospective hires. If your employment brand doesn't have the same allure for candidates as your consumer brand does for clients, it will be harder to attract the best people.

2. Recruiting and retention is, like everything else, an extension of your culture. Make sure your core values are reflected in the recruitment strategy, as well. Target people for hire who will fit well within the unique environment of the organization.

3. Have a recruiting strategy in place *in advance*, not when you suddenly need it. A sudden expansion or a huge new contract can create personnel shortages overnight. The business suffers when you aren't ready.

4. It's not easy, but you can lure candidates with a high asking price by touting the non-monetary advantages of working for you. Don't underestimate the value you bring to the table. It is fun and exciting to work in a growing small- or medium-size company.

Thinking Systematically:

1. Ensure that your company has a standardized recruiting process that all hiring managers follow. The more systematized your recruiting is, the smoother it will go in all areas of the company.

2. Establish standard procedures for conducting interviews. Train hiring managers adequately. Keep their skills refreshed and up to date as hiring practices and corporate norms evolve over the years.

3. The onboarding regimen should also be systematized, based on a clear, logical set of written procedures and actions to take from the moment the individual accepts a job offer. Each new employee should be clear on all duties and expectations before he or she even walks in the door.

CHAPTER FIVE

Strategy #3: Compensation, Recognition, and Rewards

MORE THAN A PAYCHECK

Today's workers are looking for opportunities that will allow them to grow and develop. They want to be challenged, to make a difference, and to feel appreciated. And they're looking for more than a paycheck. That's why a strategic compensation and reward system is a critical part of the human capital strategy. It's one of the most powerful tools for driving business results. Not only can it inspire employees to perform at their best, it may also be a deciding factor in whether a new employee joins your organization—or whether a top performer leaves.

When it comes to compensation and rewards, company goals should be aligned with the employee-reward system to incentivize the kind of behavior that advances the organization's long-term strategy.

Reward systems always affect employee behavior—but note that the impact can be good or bad, so be sure to design it carefully in a way that encourages the kind of behavior you desire. Employees "internalize" the system as they quickly determine how people get raises, promotions, and recognition, and their performance at work will reflect this.

Compensation Philosophy

Establishing the organization's compensation philosophy is the first and most important step in figuring out a compensation system that works. A compensation philosophy is a statement that clearly outlines how and why the organization plans to pay and reward employees based on certain performance indicators. It should specify all of the company's compensation and reward components, business objectives, and of course it should reflect the company's culture (its mission and values).

Here are a few of the essential compensation factors to consider:

- **Market competitiveness**: Is it a priority to compete for talent with other companies in the same industry?

- **Affordability**: Can the organization afford to pay competitive salaries based on fixed or base pay? If not, can additional variable pay in the form of incentives or bonuses be offered in lieu of or supplementary to a competitive base pay?

- **Strategic neutrality**: What positions are mission-critical to the company's operations and success and might require a stronger compensation package? Are there certain jobs that may not require competitive compensation?

- **Internal equity**: Do you have a framework for weighing the importance and relative value of jobs within your company?

- **Bonuses**: Does the company wish to reward employees who give discretionary effort above and beyond the job requirements?

- **Compliance**: How will the company ensure its compensation practices are legal and non-discriminatory?

Tying Compensation to the Core Values

When we began building Insperity, we carefully thought about the characteristics we were looking for in potential employees, and we spent a considerable amount of time ruminating on how to motivate employees, reward them, and make them feel valued and appreciated. It was important that our philosophy also reflected our mission and core values. Additionally, offering salary and benefits that would be competitive in the marketplace was another factor. Ultimately, we developed a philosophy that clearly outlined the "how" and "why" behind our compensation and reward system.

The language of that philosophy statement has changed throughout the years, but the essential function remains the same: to handle compensation in a way that accords with—reinforces, in fact—our values. The end result is the following compensation-philosophy statement, which has served us well:

Insperity is committed to attracting, motivating, retaining, and encouraging long-term employment of individuals with a demonstrated commitment to integrity and exemplary personal standards of performance. The Insperity culture is based upon the value of and respect for each indi-

vidual, encouraging personal and professional growth, rewarding out-standing individual and corporate performance, and achieving excellence through a high-energy, fun work environment. These elements contribute to the vision of Insperity to be an "employer of choice," which increases the value and potential of the company for all stakeholders. To this end, Insperity adheres to the following compensation strategy:

- *Establish and maintain a performance-driven culture that generates company growth by recognizing and rewarding employees who believe in their own ability to reach and exceed their compensation objectives.*

- *As part of our competitive compensation program, Insperity's base salary system will compensate employees based upon job responsibilities, level of experience, individual performance, and comparisons to the market and internal compari-sons. Additionally, we will provide an annual merit increase program to stay competitive with the market based upon employee performance, with care to avoid a high level of fixed cost escalation.*

- *Provide substantial upside for recognition and reward of individual and corporate performance through a variable pay component that is affordable and equitable to both employees and shareholders and directly supports business objectives.*

- *Create a strong mutuality of interest between executives and shareholders through the use of long-term incentive compensa-tion opportunities and the selection of business performance criteria that will result in the attainment of strategic objectives.*

- *Provide a competitive benefits package at the best possible value to the company that recognizes and encourages work-life balance and fosters a career commitment to Insperity.*

- *All employment opportunities and compensation decisions will be made in a consistent and non-discriminatory manner, without regard to race, sex, religion, age, disability, sexual orientation or marital status. To ensure this philosophy is carried out, policies and training for supervisors and managers are in place to foster consistency in practice with minimal exceptions.*

Each systematic part of our philosophy clearly states how Insperity intends to compensate and reward employees. And this philosophy statement is available to employees in the company's handbook to ensure it's always accessible.

Integrity. Respect. High-energy. Fun. It's noteworthy that the compensation philosophy starts with these key adjectives, before even mentioning things like salary and benefits. If you want to create a workplace where people are driven by more than just their paycheck, or the prospect of a raise down the line, then start with *values*. Every company pays a wage; some pay lavishly. But few can say they've built a workforce where integrity and respect form the basis for why people choose to work there.

In truth, when you get down to the specifics of the compensation philosophy, most of this stuff is pretty basic—there's nothing particularly revolutionary in ours. And that's kind of the point: you don't need to be groundbreaking, you just need a system that is clear, straightforward, and principled. In that way, you can standardize the entire organization's approach to compensation in a way that keeps all parties happy and upholds the culture you want to build.

Establishing Base Pay

When it comes to determining how much to pay employees, business leaders should research what competitors are paying for similar positions. Salary survey information is readily available today; use it to do a comparative analysis and come up with base-pay ranges with a minimum, midpoint, and maximum salary for each position. This kind of process helps you to maintain a competitive edge over other companies that candidates may be considering. In our own company, we use a wage and salary grading system. Each job is graded in accord with its respective job description, skills, and responsibilities. Then, various job titles are assigned a grade classification, and a grade scale is created for every job in the organization, from entry-level positions up to the CEO role.

Compensation ranges are assigned to each grade, weighted against comparable positions in other firms, so we can gauge our competitiveness within the market. This method ensures we are paying the right salary for each person.

As part of our salary administrative program, an annual benchmarking is conducted of almost one-third of our corporate salaried positions against other competitors in the field. Examining these same positions year over year allows us to stay current with the latest trends and offer a fair, desirable salary while staying within our budget.

Note that in some cases, it's actually prudent to pay below market rate for positions with less relative utility within *your* organization. In other words, what might be valuable in the marketplace as a whole may not be so essential in your firm. Or maybe the job is important,

Very few companies can pay at or above market for every job in their company.

but you can find someone in your company who can do it already, without having to create a new position. This is critical because very few companies can pay at or above market for every job in their company. Take a good look at what your pivotal roles are—the roles most critical to the firm's success. Offer top dollar when you need to, but don't throw away money on jobs that can be filled for less.

Sales Compensation

Salespeople are a different breed than most: they're motivated by thrill of the kill. Commissions are a powerful way of rewarding top salespeople, but there's always the question of how to balance commission with base pay. There's really no magic formula that answers this, but in our company, we align our needs with the sales team's aspirations—when we do well, they do well, and vice versa.

However, while an effective incentive plan for the sales staff can drive desired results, sales compensation also provides a good example of how the best of intentions can go awry. Salespeople have a thorough understanding of how a company's compensation system works. After all, their livelihood depends on it. And if there's a way for sales staff to take advantage of the compensation program—to game the system, in other words—they'll find it: it's human nature.

One client company instituted a new commission system to motivate its sales team and drum up new business. Under the plan, the sales representatives were eligible to earn monthly payouts based on a commission schedule, which provided graduated payout rates for ascending increments of monthly sales volume.

The system seemed to be effective. After a few months, sales had indeed increased, but management discovered an irregularity in the sales pattern. Some of these sales representatives were "hoarding" their sales from one month to the next to secure a higher commission rate under the graduated schedule. As a result, it was creating overpayments to these reps and causing undesired fluctuations in the client's monthly revenues.

Insperity's experts helped the firm redesign the commission plan to preempt overpayments and discourage sales tricks. The revised plan was documented and distributed to the sales staff, who were probably a little disappointed they couldn't "game the system" anymore, but they were still rewarded for their sales numbers. As a result, this new strategy led to a more consistent pattern of sales performance while maintaining the revenue boost encouraged by the commission system.

Incentive Compensation

Variable-pay or incentive compensation offers employees the opportunity to earn a bonus above their base pay for achieving certain individual or team results. It can also encourage employees to focus on particular team or company goals. Incentive pay works best when the company's leaders establish clearly defined, measurable objectives that parallel the overall company strategy. When managers effectively link compensation to critical projects and timelines, improvement in key metrics in sales or service, or achieving set financial benchmarks, it can help the company make great strides toward its goals.

In our early days, Insperity established an annual incentive-compensation plan that aligns the incentive pay with the company's goals for the year. Although it's a fairly laborious process that entails resetting the goals based on the upcoming year's objectives, it motivates individual performance and reinforces the notion that each employee has a stake in the success of the organization as a whole. We sink or swim together. All for one, one for all.

The table below illustrates Insperity's annual incentive plan. What works for us might not necessarily work for you, but use it as an example of how compensation can be effectively tied to a few personal, division, and corporate benchmarks.

Annual Incentive Program for a Management-Level Position

Measurement type	Incentive plan component	GOAL			
		Threshold 50% of target payout)	Target (100% of target payout)	Stretch (150% of target payout)	Maximum (200% of target payout)
Corporate	Corporate objectives (50%)	$____	$____	$____	$____
Division	Division objectives (30%)	$____	$____	N/A	N/A
Individual	Personal contributions (20%)	$____	$____	N/A	$____

As the chart shows, the potential payout for each measurement type is defined as a percentage of the target payout. Depending on the employee's position in the company, individual contributions can have a greater impact at the division or corporate level. This chart illustrates a typical management-level incentive program, which offers a higher percentage of the bonus potential based on "division objectives" and "corporate objectives." This reflects how a management role in the company carries more responsibility for ensuring that the division and the company meet their annual goals. At the other end of the spectrum, entry-level positions tend to be more heavily weighted toward their personal contributions and less so toward the corporate and division goals.

Long-Term Incentives

Other aspects of compensation every business should evaluate are long-term incentives. Leaders should first determine whether such an arrangement is suitable to the business and take note of the difference between employees having a long-term view of their role and the company's success, as opposed to actually possessing an ownership mentality, which typically requires a greater level of commitment.

It's not a given that every company will be better off if all employees have an ownership mentality. An ownership mentality can greatly benefit individual performance but can also stymie company agility, risk tolerance, and profitability. An effective strategy in this area is based upon an accurate analysis of the level of long-term commitment required or desired for employees throughout the organization. This analysis becomes the primary consideration whether equity or cash compensation is the best form of long-term compensation.

Since our company's early days, I've been a big fan of stock options—under the right circumstances, and for the right reasons. In the past, we found that employees' views toward stock ownership varied widely. Some just saw it is as another form of cash compensation and liquidated their shares as soon as they had the chance to do so. That's not reflective of a true ownership mentality and it doesn't cultivate a sense of long-term commitment—a "we're all in this together" spirit that leader-entrepreneurs should build.

When you own a business, you've put so much on the line and have invested your blood, sweat, and tears (not to mention your savings). Protect the equity you've built. I think owners often undervalue their creation, as surprising as that may seem. They're too quick to sell or give away stakes in the company in their drive to get where they want to go. Consider taking steps toward extending ownership benefit instead of giving up equity too soon. For example: a plan for sharing a portion of the profits of the company offers an "ownership-like" benefit but avoids the complication of equity compensation. It doesn't mean you shouldn't give up equity under certain circumstances—but weigh the decision carefully.

Benefits

Employee benefits play as much of a role as base pay in recruiting and retention. Health care, retirement plans, and other sources of financial security are important factors that people consider in their choice of employer. Of course, benefits can be pricey, and they tend to be cost-volatile from year to year. Therefore, a careful analysis of how much to spend on benefits, and how to spend it, is critical.

In many companies, the employee benefits package isn't the product of a carefully designed plan; it's just a hodgepodge of perks that have evolved over the years. When it comes to benefits, you must think strategically—put your resources where they'll have the most impact.

Of course, figuring out what to spend, when, and on whom quickly becomes highly complex and technical. Insurance programs, for example, are intricate and confusing, and deciding on a seemingly infinite number of choices can vex even the most patient entrepreneurs. Business owners constantly fret over the escalating costs of insurance and other benefits. Controlling these expenses and getting the best value for your workforce is a daunting challenge for small- to medium-sized companies. One of the most valued services Insperity provides to its clients is professional, sophisticated benefits administration that eliminates the complexity, minimizes the compliance burden, and keeps costs in line with your budget.

Another way Insperity helps businesses with benefits issues is by simply encouraging their employees to take advantage of the benefits already available to them. In many companies, benefits are underutilized, or employees aren't aware of what's offered.

One of the biggest sources of frustration among small- and medium-sized business owners is that they feel they can't compete with larger competitors when it comes to the benefits package. Insperity levels the playing field in that respect.

A husband and wife are long-time Insperity clients who run an IT outsourcing company for small businesses. As a small business themselves (with fewer than twenty employees), it's a challenge to attract job applicants who might also be applying to tech behemoths like Google or Dell.

The owner of the company says that they lure talented people, "by telling the story of our culture, it's infectious. People wanna come here and be part of our team. And we have to care for our employees, they have to feel deeply cared for. And Insperity has enabled us to create a benefits package that cares deeply for our people … With Insperity, we have access to the tools that the big boys have."

Fairness vs. Equity

Calibrating the "right" salary for every employee in every position is a difficult task. Most employees believe their compensation is unfair: *"They make too much, and I make too little."* People want to be treated fairly, and leaders certainly don't want anyone to feel slighted. So why do so many employees believe their compensation is unjust?

When it comes to compensation, "fairness" is the wrong goal to pursue. It's too subjective and vague. The most successful compensation strategies establish compensation levels based upon more objective criteria.

For example, an effective base-pay program includes a wage and salary structure that compares pay levels for similar jobs at other companies in the same industry and geographical location. It also analyzes the comparative value of different roles based on how essential they are and how much they contribute to the organization as a whole. Not all employees have the same job, nor should they necessarily be paid the same. Ultimately, for any job, the answer to the question "Why is my base pay X dollars?" can be explained by conducting an objective analysis of the value of that specific role within the company.

This concept is referred to as *internal equity*, and it's an objective and dependable means of figuring out who gets paid what.

Consider the following case study. A nonprofit client company was suffering from poor employee morale and low productivity, because employees felt their pay was unfair. Management didn't have any idea how to address these complaints, short of giving everyone a lavish raise, which would have been a poor solution to the problem even if it were financially viable—which it wasn't.

After helping the company develop a compensation philosophy, Insperity service providers worked with the client to produce a job-evaluation system. This required translating the various duties, tasks, and responsibilities into varying levels of compensable factors. For example, factors such as "problem-solving," "decision-making," and "customer influence" existed in varying degrees in all jobs throughout the organization. In order to compare the value of different positions, the client had to rate each factor and then weigh the aggregate contributive value of each job. Jobs were grouped together by total points to establish pay grades, which were assigned a salary range. The client company also benchmarked positions against other companies of its size, industry, and location.

By applying this methodical, objective process, the company's leadership was able to calculate the relative worth of each job based on the sum of the points across factors—a much better method than, say, arbitrarily assigning a dollar amount based on a vague set of criteria in one's head.

In the end, the client company was in a strong position to make the wage adjustments necessary for the different positions. And management was in a better position to handle questions about pay by pointing to a specific set of criteria, which made the whole salary process less opaque and ultimately improved employee morale and retention. Frustrating conversations about fairness, which are always riddled with subjectivity and arbitrariness, gave way to clear communications and objective criteria.

It's not a perfect science, and it still requires making certain value judgments, but it freed the organization's managers of the maddening task of determining compensation levels, plus it resolved the longstanding frustration among the workers about their pay.

Employee Recognition and Appreciation

A recognition and appreciation program that formally acknowledges excellent employees for their hard work is a low-cost part of a compensation plan, but one that offers a high return on investment— especially when it comes to motivating employees. And when you tie it into the company's mission and values, it fosters the culture you're trying to build.

Feeling recognized and appreciated meets a deep emotional need that we all have. Have you ever heard someone complain, "I am treated more like a number than a person"? People don't do their best work when they feel like faceless, nameless cogs in the wheel. They want to know that their work is meaningful and important, and to have their supervisors and colleagues recognize it as such. That doesn't mean the company should bestow awards on every warm body just for walking through the door; participation ribbons don't work in the real world. But it does mean that hard work and team contributions should be recognized as such.

When the leadership implements a plan to demonstrate genuine appreciation for their people, employees engage in a higher level of discretionary effort, which should be a major objective for any effective human capital strategy. Discretionary effort occurs when employees go beyond what is expected of them when no one is looking. It often entails a higher level of creativity and problem solving—with a greater level of commitment and energy—that employees exercise when they know they are appreciated.

I've spoken a little bit about Insperity's recognition program. It's an important feature of our culture, and a highlight of sales conventions, the fall kickoff event, and other large corporate gatherings. It's one of the things that make us stand out from the pack, and probably has a lot to do with our regular appearance on "best places to work" lists. In truth, I can't imagine an effective style of corporate leadership that *doesn't* involve trumpeting people's accomplishments. Good leaders don't just issue orders, make rules, and whip people into shape. They make people feel valued. They show appreciation. They make their people feel like part of a family.

One of the most amazing parts of a consistent employee recognition plan is that showing gratitude doesn't have to be expensive; in fact, it doesn't have to cost anything at all. Demonstrating true appreciation toward others is a skill that can and should be taught to executives, supervisors, and managers, and also encouraged among regular employees, since peer recognition is often as powerful as being recognized by the boss. Executives often underestimate the power of a thank you, a simple note acknowledging extra effort, or a compliment for a job well done. Showing appreciation is simply making sure people know that what they do is important and noticed. It's an essential component of any human capital strategy.

Thinking Strategically:

1. Don't deal with compensation in isolation from the other aspects of your business. Your compensation strategy must be aligned with your overall corporate strategy. Articulating a clear and concise compensation philosophy is an effective way of evaluating this alignment. Similarly, your compensation practices should be congruent with your company culture.

2. Evaluate your total rewards system including compensation, benefits, flexible scheduling, PTO, and recognition.

3. Compensation is not the *only* factor in encouraging employees to go the extra mile, but it is a strong one. Conversely, if your people seem to just be putting in the bare minimum, it could be a product of inadequate— or unevenly distributed—compensation. What should you change as a result? Look at discretionary effort as a barometer of an effective rewards system.

Thinking Systematically:

1. Figuring out compensation should be more science than art. There's no perfectly objective means of determining who should get paid what, but there are certain methodologies you can apply that can establish fair pay ranges for each position in line with what your competitors are offering.

2. Base pay, incentive compensation, commissions—they're all viable compensation options that drive behavior and performance. And don't overlook benefits as an enticing part of your compensation package and as an opportunity to show how much you care for employees and their families. Helping employees avail themselves of the full range of benefits will, by extension, help the company too.

3. Develop a consistent recognition program and use it as an opportunity to show genuine appreciation for your people.

CHAPTER SIX

Strategy #4: Compliance and Liability Management

PLAYING DEFENSE

Most entrepreneurs decide to go into business for themselves because they want to be their own bosses. As an entrepreneur myself, I understand the satisfaction that comes from owning a business: the freedom to make all of the decisions, and the financial and personal rewards that come along with it. But with this ownership comes a great responsibility. Almost every decision a business owner makes involves the prospect of immense, and sometimes dire, repercussions.

Employers have an enormous list of obligations, responsibilities, and liabilities that can interfere with the business depending on how the day-to-day operations of the organization are managed. This also holds true for *anyone* in the organization in a leadership or management role. From the moment the first employee is recruited, to how that individual is compensated, promoted, disciplined, and terminated, every decision and action can and will be scrutinized— and possibly misconstrued. And when that happens, the potential for liability increases tenfold, generating a risk of large fines or litigation that can cost hundreds of thousands of dollars, indeterminable hours of lost productivity, and sometimes the business itself.

When the topic of paying fines and employer-related lawsuits comes up, business owners often say, "It's never happened to us." Entrepreneurs, particularly SMB owners (an inherently optimistic lot), sometimes assume they won't be held to the same set of standards or responsibilities as their larger counterparts. They tend to think they'll never be audited or hit with a lawsuit. Unfortunately, it *does* happen, and it *can* happen at any time and to any business. And the reality is that it's even *more* critical for smaller companies that usually lack the deep pockets and in-house legal teams of the big guys.

Not only are employer-compliance and liability issues costly and time-consuming, they're also emotionally draining and can negatively affect employee morale and productivity. Employers who operate on an "out of sight, out of mind" attitude will only make matters worse by leaving themselves unprepared and vulnerable to risks. Nothing can interrupt the momentum in a workplace quite like the sudden need to respond to regulatory or legal problems. And the emotional toll that a claim or lawsuit takes on business leaders can be devastating.

Businesses can mitigate the risk with a well-developed compliance and liability-management strategy. And that begins with establishing a positive company culture and creating guidelines and policies designed to *prevent* inappropriate or illegal conduct that leads to messy legal actions. In our many years of managing companies' human capital issues, we've found that the preventive approach is the best: avoid problems before they even start. In this way, Insperity has helped its client companies save millions of dollars every year and dodge unnecessary emotional stress and loss in productivity.

New Government Regulations Since 1900

Regulations in 1900	Regulations in 1960	Regulations in 1980	Regulations today
			PPACA
			HCEARA
			AHRA
			HRE
			GINA
			HEART
			MHPAEA
			WRERA
			PPA
			AJCA
			MMA
			EGTRRA
			WHCRRA
			TRA '97
			SBJPA
			HIPAA
			MHPA
			NMHPA
			USERRA
			URA
			FMLA
			UCA
			ADA
			DFWA
			IRCA
			TRA '86
			COBRA
			DEFRA
			REA
			TEFRA
		PDA	PDA
		ERISA	ERISA
		OSHA	OSHA
		ADEA	ADEA
		CRA	CRA
	FUTA	FUTA	FUTA
	FLSA	FLSA	FLSA
	FICA	FICA	FICA
	NLCA	NLCA	NLCA
COMMON LAW	COMMON LAW	COMMON LAW	COMMON LAW
CASE LAW	CASE LAW	CASE LAW	CASE LAW
LOCAL LAWS	LOCAL LAWS	LOCAL LAWS	LOCAL LAWS
STATE LAWS	STATE LAWS	STATE LAWS	STATE LAWS

What is this alphabet soup of legal mumbo jumbo? Most business owners won't be familiar with all of these acronyms, which constitute just a few of the overwhelming number of government regulations that employers are required to adhere to every day. Unfortunately, most entrepreneurs, especially first-time owners, don't grasp the multitude of regulations and how those regulations impact their own business. Even entrepreneurs who follow employment practices and try to do the right thing are often caught off guard. It really takes a specialist to make sense of it all. It's not something that busy entrepreneurs with their eyes to the future should get bogged down in trying to figure out.

Although these laws are sometimes burdensome, they do play an important role in creating a healthy working environment for all Americans. Federal laws such as Title VII, Americans with Disabilities Act (ADA), Fair Labor Standards Act (FLSA), and the Family and Medical Leave Act (FMLA) have been developed over the years in an effort to provide certain safeguards and guarantees.

Nonetheless, given that not just federal but state and local governments are adopting more and more laws and regulations, the regulatory landscape can seem like an impenetrable mess. And the number of employment-related regulations has nearly *tripled* since the 1980s. Not only are the laws continuing to grow at a rapid pace, but they're also constantly changing, which makes it challenging for business owners to keep up.

Maintaining compliance is a proactive, rather than reactive, activity. Companies that stay on top of government regulations—and show a good-faith effort to follow them—win the day over businesses that ignore this area, cross their fingers, and hope their noncompliance goes unnoticed. Trust me—the costs and aggravation that can come from dealing with a recovery effort to maintain compliance are more difficult and costlier to overcome than the burden of maintaining compliance in the first place.

As the HR department for thousands of client companies, we've made it our mission to keep up with the growing and constantly changing laws. By following the HR practices highlighted in this book, and anticipating problematic situations that might occur, our organization has been fortunate to maintain a strong compliance and liability-management strategy based on a thorough set of practices, policies, and procedures to which we adhere diligently.

Types of Employment Risks

There are three types of potential employment risks that businesses face: regulatory exposure, civil exposure, and criminal exposure.

Regulatory Exposure

Regulatory exposure refers to the fines and fees a business must pay for violating local, state, or federal laws. These aren't criminal laws, but the vast body of regulations governing everything from personal medical privacy (HIPAA) to wage and hour requirements. At any given time and without notice, a government agency can audit a company's employment practices, which may include its benefits administration, pay practices, and safety and records management. If the agency determines that the business isn't compliant, the employer is hit with one or more penalties. Additionally, the company is responsible for making the necessary changes required to meet regulatory standards. Complaints and claims can be filed by anyone—a current or former employee, a potential new hire, or even a vendor or a customer. And companies can be audited more than once.

Civil Exposure

A disgruntled employee decides to sue you for wrongful termination. A manager claims discrimination after being passed over for a promotion. A group of employees claim they should have been paid overtime. The number of pitfalls is endless.

Civil exposure refers to the fines and/or compensable damages that a business owner may incur from a lawsuit. It involves paying legal fees and any potential damages that may be awarded in a lawsuit. Sometimes employers may be hit with both a regulatory-related penalty *and* a lawsuit for the same offense. For example, an employee may file a harassment claim with the Equal Employment Opportunity Commission *and* individually sue the employer.

Of course, incorporating your business offers several protections against liability, namely that it safeguards your personal assets and keeps them separate from liability or debt incurred by the company. But it doesn't protect you *individually* from any actions you might take either as an employer, as a trustee, as a plan sponsor, or a host of other roles into which you are thrust as an employer. Therefore, you can encounter all kinds of civil exposure that has nothing to do with what your corporate structure is.

This area of compliance is a minefield, and a lot of owners want to pretend it doesn't exist. It's one of the most powerful things we do for our clients since we relieve them of the burden of having to be a plan sponsor or trustee, and thus we spare them a great deal of risk.

Criminal Exposure

In addition to paying regulatory fines and/or civil penalties, failure to comply with some employment-related statutes may also subject an employer and/or company officers to criminal penalties. This can especially happen to repeat offenders. For example, employers who continue to hire undocumented immigrants may be hit with fines, but they may also face imprisonment. An employer who doesn't pay wages to employees can be subjected to criminal charges and may serve time in prison if convicted—in addition to the painful prospect of a civil lawsuit. And similar to personal tax evasion, employers and/ or company officers who fail to pay the company's taxes may owe back taxes *and* be charged criminally.

Minimizing and Managing Risks: Establishing a Strong Foundation

Remember, being proactive in compliance is the best approach. Prevention is better than the cure. In this way, employers are better positioned to protect themselves, their employees, and the business.

Cultivate the Right Culture

Yes, that's right—culture again! The culture is truly the foundation of a strong human capital strategy, and that also applies to compliance and liability management. If your culture's values are articulated clearly, and if they have been made part of the fabric of the organization rather than just relegated to empty sloganeering, they provide a strong preventive buffer against the ever-present threat of liability. The reason is simple: a business with a culture that encourages ethical behavior and a positive atmosphere is less likely to run afoul of the law.

One of Insperity's values is respecting the worth of the individual. In the way we operate internally, and in how we assist client companies with resolving their own personnel issues, respect for the individual is demonstrated and reinforced in everything we do. This kind of attitude minimizes many employer-related risks, since of course many employee complaints originate from feeling disrespected or maltreated.

Toxic workplaces produce toxic results. But positive, supportive environments foster respect and integrity. Set a good example, and others will follow suit. It's not just the right thing to do; it will protect you and your business.

The Employee Handbook

This, too, is essential! Don't skimp on the employee handbook. Employees should regard it as a foundational document, not just something to be shoved into the back of one's desk drawer after glancing through it on their first day of work. Consider it your human capital bible.

An employee handbook, more likely an online document than an actual printed book, serves to bridge any gaps between the employees' and the company's expectations while encouraging adherence to company protocols. In the early days at Insperity, we just published a supervisor handbook that contained the company's policies and procedures. Eventually, we realized that the handbook is indispensable for all members of the company, not just supervisors. Today, employees are also required to sign an acknowledgement documenting that they've received a copy of the handbook and understand its contents.

The employee handbook should be issued to new employees as soon as possible to speed their acclimation to the company's policies and procedures. Consequently, distributing the handbook is a key part of our new-employee orientation. And employers should treat it as a living document, which means updating it regularly and communicating any changes to all employees.

Obviously, each organization's handbook will be different, but the most common topics that a handbook should cover include:

- Company Mission

- Company Core Values

- Conduct

  - Acceptable Conduct

  - Anti-Harassment Policy

  - Code of Business Conduct and Ethics

  - Drug Free Workplace Policy

  - Weapons

  - Employee Complaint Procedures

  - Personal Appearance

  - Post-Accident Testing, if applicable

  - Safe Workplace

  - Safety and Health

- Communications

  - Confidentiality Policy

  - Confidentiality of Sensitive Personal Information, if applicable

  - Overview of Americans with Disabilities Act (ADA)

  - Disclosure Policy

  - Social Media Policy

  - Use of Computers and Communication Systems Policy (including Cyber)

- Compensation
  - Employee Compensation Overview
  - Salary Administration (wage and hourly policy)
- Employee Absence
  - Accommodation of Disabilities
  - California (CA) Paid Time Off (PTO), if applicable
  - Holiday(s)
  - Leaves of Absence
  - Paid Time Off (PTO)
- Employment
  - Complaint Resolution
  - Equal Employment Opportunity
  - Hours of Work
  - New Employee Onboarding
  - Performance Appraisal
  - Termination of Employment
- Hiring
  - Hiring Practices
  - Relocation, if applicable
- Travel and Expense
  - Employee Business Expenses Policy and Process

Liability-Management Training

One of the most cost-effective preventative measures business owners can take is to offer liability-management training for supervisors and employees. This can range from supervisory training on managing conflicts to anti-harassment and anti-discrimination training for all employees. Such training also reinforces the company's culture by supporting the behaviors that are congruent with its values.

Don't underestimate the impact of liability-management training. It might seem redundant—after all, everyone understands that discrimination is wrong and generally illegal, right? But the topic can be more complicated than meets the eye.

For example, actions that constitute discrimination might not be overt or intentional. Supervisors and employees may be blithely unaware they're running afoul of the law. Educating your workforce helps prevent ugly disputes (and potential lawsuits) before they arise.

Liability training—particularly anti-discrimination and anti-harassment education—is one of the most beneficial preventative measures and provides the greatest defense for a company when it's conducted annually. Our corporate employees participate in an annual renewal class online designed to re-educate them on existing policies and expected behaviors while at work. It also strengthens our culture. The rewards greatly exceed the financial and time cost of running these trainings.

We've enabled thousands of client companies to steer clear of fines and lawsuits by shoring up their anti-discrimination and anti-harassment procedures. For example, when one of our client companies experienced a rise in Equal Employment Opportunity complaints, we helped them implement a robust training program and advised them on modifying some of their workplace policies.

Following these measures, the complaints decreased by 25 percent in two years.

Follow Good Hiring Practices

As I talked about in chapter four, recruiting the right person in the first place is the best way to avoid headaches down the road. And that, of course, means hiring not just on the basis of skill but also on character and personality, too. Beware of job candidates and employees with a perpetually negative attitude—often, they're the ones who cause trouble.

Fortunately, you don't have to be an FBI profiler to figure out the kind of person an interviewee really is. Background checks should be a standard part of the hiring process. But many employers don't know or choose to ignore proper and lawful procedures in this area. For example, if an employer decides to conduct background checks, it must be done fairly and consistently. This requires administering background checks to *all* of the job candidates to avoid possible discrimination claims. Additionally, employment applications and background forms must be accurate and complete to avoid potential risks and liabilities. That may sound like stating the obvious, but you'd be surprised at how easy it is to forget a vital form or check a certain box, especially for small businesses overburdened with HR tasks.

In the midst of the growing and ever-changing regulations on background checks, it's a constant quest to continue to educate our clients. Fortunately, we've designed ways to help our client companies streamline background-check processes, and we have compliance specialists who can navigate the labyrinthine ins and outs of the regulatory landscape. These are also the same guidelines Insperity follows in its own corporate hiring practices.

Here's an example of why specialized expertise is necessary for this particularly complex area of human capital management. Some years ago, after Insperity handled a background check on a highly qualified job candidate for a client company, it was revealed that this individual had several past criminal convictions. Understandably, the client was concerned and wanted to steer clear of any future problems, so they decided not to hire the candidate. However, the company didn't realize that passing on this otherwise qualified individual opened the firm up to potential charges. As is the case in many decisions an employer makes, both options have risks and require a deeper analysis to make the right decision.

Insperity worked closely to educate the client on anti-discriminatory hiring laws and to learn more about the convictions, which turned out to be non-job-related and happened a long time ago. After evaluating all of the facts and questions of law, the client decided the risk of hiring the ex-offender was minimal compared to the disastrous impact of a potential discrimination claim and/or a lawsuit. Ultimately, it worked out for both parties, as the new hire proved to be one of the company's most productive and successful employees.

Drug Testing

Drug testing is another area that is fraught with risk. Drug testing may be part of a pre-employment process, be randomly administered to existing employees, or applied selectively to individuals in specific cases, such as post-accident testing. However, as with background checks, there exists a bevy of laws governing who can be drug tested, when, and under what circumstances. It's risky business to try to engage in drug testing without a full understanding of the relevant laws.

For example, a client owner with employees in multiple locations was informed that some employees were using drugs while at work. The client company wanted to immediately begin random drug testing of its workforce. However, they weren't aware that in order to legitimately conduct random drug testing, a comprehensive substance-abuse policy must be in place, and all employees at each worksite must sign an agreement consenting to the testing. Furthermore, the selection process must be conducted randomly. With assistance from Insperity's drug-testing specialists, the client was properly guided to follow these required procedures and executed a successful—and legal—random drug-testing process.

Managing Employee Performance

Sometimes, even the best employees experience—or cause—angst. Whether an organization is comprised of two employees or thousands, issues and disputes will arise. An employee might feel underpaid compared to a coworker or resent being passed over for a promotion. Or a supervisor's constructive feedback, which was only intended to motivate the employee to do better, might be interpreted as unadulterated criticism. By taking precautions and following good performance-management practices, company leaders may be able to prevent an employee from claiming unfair treatment based on discrimination, a disability, or even excessive absences.

Planning for the worst in business is a necessity, not an option. Prudent management requires understanding that conflict is going to happen. Our corporate-conflict plan is the same model we implement and customize according to our client companies' needs. The goal is always the same: to resolve the issue *before* it escalates to a filed claim or potential lawsuit.

Communication is the pressure valve that eases conflict before it explodes. Emotions can trigger many employees to file complaints. Offering employees a safe outlet to air their grievances helps mediate their personal reactions and encourages them to work to remedy problematic situations without turning to outside resources for resolution. Establishing guidelines and policies early on allows employees to defuse conflicts as soon as they happen. Often, employees can resolve the problem without the involvement of a supervisor or HR representative.

Open and honest communication means that supervisors must be willing to confront performance issues, not avoid them. Employees need to be informed and given forewarning when they're not performing their duties as expected. They should be able to recognize when they're meeting company standards and when their job may be in jeopardy. An employee should never be surprised by a termination, which, except in rare cases, should only occur after a series of meetings to discuss the problem. Otherwise, it's a poor reflection on the supervisor who failed to properly and effectively manage the performance problems before they reached a breaking point.

We promote an open-door policy that encourages employees to talk to their supervisor—or any supervisor within the company—about any concerns. This approach has helped many employees settle matters by giving them an opportunity to sort through problems and come up with solutions. And when necessary, our corporate HR team is available (on a confidential basis) to assist in communicating the issues and resolving concerns with all parties involved. Providing these healthy outlets for employees minimizes the risk of potential litigation or claims.

Managing difficult employees is really a special skill unto itself, one that requires that right balance of firmness, empathy, and dialogue. We've identified four common types of problematic employees: the overly emotional person, the bully, the naysayer (someone who is perpetually negative and cynical), and the social butterfly. As you might expect, each situation is dealt with differently, but the common thread in handling all four types is calm, non-confrontational communication. Focus on the *behavior*, not the person, in the process of working out a solution.

In addition, conducting regular performance reviews (discussed in greater detail in the next chapter) and having an employee grievance policy are effective ways of minimizing the impact of difficult people.

The longer you spend at the helm, the better you'll get at reading people, handling their issues, and mediating disagreements among colleagues. That's not to say that these things will overwhelm your daily schedule or preclude you from doing what you do best, which is running and growing a company. But it just means that, as we said before, "behavioral scientist" is one of many hats you must wear. In return, you'll be rewarded by your employees, who will see that the person at the top empathizes with their concerns, wants them to do well, and is willing to work hard to create a supportive environment for them each day.

Termination: The Last Resort

Wrongful termination is a serious risk for employers, and it's easy for a business leader to think their reasons for firing an employee are valid without realizing they're in violation of some obscure law. Termination should only happen as a last resort, and only after following certain procedures to try to rectify the problem. In this way, businesses avoid potentially devastating claims and litigation.

First, documentation is key. Documenting important actions such as employee disputes, disciplinary measures, and discussions about performance protect an employer against wrongful-termination claims. Supervisors should maintain detailed notes on any actions that were implemented to try to remedy the issue.

Second, if problems persist, consider developing a performance improvement plan (PIP) for the employee. This is a formalized approach to bettering the employee's bad behavior. The PIP should enumerate what the problem areas are and specify goals to correct them. The goals should also be accompanied by a timeline for achieving them.

Specificity is key here. Make sure both parties understand and agree on the terms. For example, a PIP for a chronically tardy worker might state:

John Doe will arrive at work before the start of each work shift and clock in on or before his start time. He will promptly return from scheduled break times and work until the end of each shift. Improvement needs to be immediate, marked, and sustained. Failure to work all scheduled shifts in their entirety or continued punctuality issues could result in discipline up to and including termination.

Or, if the employee exhibits a deficiency in work skills, the PIP might say something like:

Sally Brown has been submitting reports with numerous grammatical, spelling, and technical errors. Within the next thirty days, Sally needs to complete Business Writing 101, as well as utilize grammar and spell checking tools prior to submitting reports. Technical data should be reviewed by the Engineering group. We will meet again next Tuesday to review progress.

When all else fails and every option has been exhausted, termination may be the best resolution for both the employer and employee. Prior to terminating your employee, be sure to review all relevant documentation and confer with your legal counsel or HR representative. Confirm that you're abiding by all state-specific wage and hour regulations. If you're using employment contracts or non-compete/

non-solicitation agreements, make sure your legal counsel provides you with validity and enforcement guidance.

When the time comes to sit down with the employee and formally terminate their employment, supervisors should maintain professionalism and focus on the facts—don't make the termination personal. At the same time, be candid about the reasons—don't misidentify the termination as a "layoff" or the firm "going in a different direction," and don't ask the employee to resign in lieu of being fired. People will respect and appreciate that you're being up front with them.

Depending on the risks at hand, a separation and release agreement can help the employer ease the burden of termination. By signing this type of formal legal document, the employee gives up certain rights and claims in exchange for additional compensation to ease the transition while looking for a new job. This agreement minimizes the chances of an employee filing a lawsuit related to employment or the termination.

The following case provides a cautionary tale on how *not* to handle this delicate issue—and why clear communication and a thorough understanding of relevant law are indispensable.

A long-time employee at a client company was starting to miss work due to migraines. Frustrated by the employee's continued absences and decline in performance, the supervisor fired the employee. As a result, the terminated employee filed a claim with the Equal Employment Opportunity Commission (EEOC) based on the employer's failure to provide a reasonable accommodation for the employee's disability.

The employer was shocked to learn that the employee's migraines were considered a disability. The employer also wasn't aware of the ADA's legal requirements to hold a conversation with the employee and to provide reasonable accommodations that might have improved the employee's performance. Unfortunately, the supervisor didn't keep any documentation on the employee's performance issues or give the employee an opportunity to tell her side of the story. Ultimately, the company was unable to defend its position, which resulted in a hefty financial penalty for the employer.

Additional Protection

Employment Practices Liability Insurance

One of the smartest decisions business leaders can make is to invest in insurance coverage. Similar to homeowner's insurance, employment practices liability insurance (EPLI) offers that extra layer of protection and peace of mind that lets owners stop worrying about all of the risks and instead focus on growing the business.

Depending on the type of claim and coverage, EPLI can minimize the exposures for some discriminatory claims, wrongful terminations, negligence, and personal injury, to name a few. Among our client companies, if an employee makes a complaint or files a charge, an Insperity Equal Employment Opportunity specialist will investigate and attempt to resolve the matter. Insperity brings an unemotional, professional, objective viewpoint to the table and offers employees an opportunity to vent their grievances. In most cases, this is enough to resolve the matter. If not, the EPLI carrier will assign an attorney to assist the client. Although some situations may not be covered under the insurance carrier, when Insperity provides assistance, our client companies have saved countless hours in time they would've otherwise spent on investigation and legal fees.

EPLI coverage usually also requires employers to implement a process to handle employee complaints. This is beneficial for business to ease the emotional burden when a conflict occurs. The last thing you want when a problem arises is a haphazard response, which can make the problem worse. For your own emotional security, establish a mechanism for responding to employee complaints.

Annual Risk Assessment

Once you institutionalize all these policies, guidelines, and practices to maintain compliance and avoid liabilities, it's important to review them and ensure each area is up to date. One of our annual management team meetings includes an analysis of the company's risks—things that can tip the boat or take us by surprise when we least expect them. Although this can be a daunting task, it's another essential weapon in the preventative arsenal.

Thinking Strategically:

1. Everything ties back into the corporate culture; compliance and liability is no exception. A strong culture that practices the values it preaches provides a sturdy coat of armor against legal liabilities.

2. Now that you understand how things can go wrong when it comes to compliance, assess the areas of greatest risk in your organization. Think long term and proactively, and devise a plan to mitigate those risks.

3. Hiring and recruiting is a strategic area with important implications for compliance and liability. You might even say it's the canary in the coal mine for personnel issues that could arise later. If you're routinely hiring negative, difficult, or uncooperative people who aren't compatible with your company's positive culture, those individuals

could cause trouble (with their colleagues, with the firm, or with you) down the road.

Thinking Systematically:

1. What process and procedure will work best in your organization to handle possible employee complaints that may arise?

2. Communication is key. Operate an open-door policy that encourages employees to talk candidly about their concerns with supervisors. Better yet, supplement it with a formal grievance-resolution policy for more serious issues.

3. Training and education are like vaccines against legal crises: they prevent the disease from even occurring in the first place. Liability-management training, anti-harassment training, and anti-discrimination training are almost always worth the cost.

4. The employee handbook is a cornerstone of your compliance and liability protocol. It ensures everyone is on the same page regarding rules and expectations, it educates new (and old) employees about what they should and should not do, and it can aid in your defense if you face a lawsuit or legal claim.

CHAPTER SEVEN

Strategy #5: Employee Performance Improvement

KNOWLEDGE RIGHTLY APPLIED

Everyone wants to know the secret of success. *What did you do? How did you do it? What can I do to achieve similar results?* Sometimes it seems like the answer is simply being at the right place at the right time. Chance is certainly part of the equation, but success is achieved when opportunity and preparedness meet. Most people succeed by working hard and pushing themselves to be the best they can be, so they are ready when the right moment comes along. They surround themselves with anything and everything that can help them. Seldom accepting the status quo, striving entrepreneurs always look for ways to improve. And the best entrepreneurs look for ways to empower *others* to improve, too.

The total performance of a company is the sum of the performance of the individuals who work within it. An effective human capital strategy should include a game plan for continuously cultivating each employee's personal talent and skills. The two most important areas of a performance-improvement strategy are performance management (accurately evaluating employees' proficiency) and training and development (honing their abilities so your people are at the top of their game).

This is another area where you must don your behavioral scientist hat. Performance management is intricately tied to personality assessment and group dynamics—how individuals do their job, and whether they lift up or hold back those around them.

For this reason, examining personality traits is a big part of how we handle performance management at Insperity. We strive to really understand the *individuals* whose names appear on the top of the performance review sheet, to consider their values and the unique way they think, to parse out what energizes and excites them. We use the DiSC assessment tool, which analyzes one's personality in terms of four component traits: dominance, influence, steadiness, and conscientiousness. You don't necessarily have to adopt the same method; find one that works for you.

Regardless of your approach, it's important to convey that the performance-management process serves to help you help them. Its function is to empower them to achieve their objectives. People can tell if an interaction with a superior at work is for the benefit of both parties, or just for the higher-up asking the questions. People generally want to please; they want to do well at work and they want to *know* they're doing well, if in fact they are. If they're not, they want to hear that too. Only then can they begin to improve. Some managers shy away from giving negative feedback. But that's a missed opportunity. Often, negative feedback is the impetus employees need to wake up and make a change. After all, one of the best things you can do as an owner is not just provide a paycheck—it's to enable people to become the best version of themselves.

Fail Fast

In most successful companies, performance improvement is part of a broader commitment to learn and improve as an organization. Companies that are devoted to learning and growing understand that failure is an opportunity to learn instead of a cause for blame.

Many people at Insperity have heard me say, "Failure is okay, but fail fast!" There's nothing wrong with making mistakes—just do it quickly, learn from it, and move forward. This natural form of learning is similar to the way a baby learns to grab a rattle. When a baby attempts to reach for a rattle the first time, the baby will reach to one side and miss. This pattern will repeat over and over until the feedback provided by the failures will allow the baby to hone in on the goal and grab the rattle. After a string of failures and a couple of successes, the baby becomes proficient at grabbing objects. So it goes with learning in the business world.

In performance improvement, the purpose trumps the process. If the goal of giving honest, accurate, and complete feedback (even if it's negative) is to facilitate personal (and, by extension, organizational) improvement, then it doesn't matter too much *how* you go about it, as long as you follow the basic principles outlined in this chapter. On the other hand, if the purpose is to call people out or nitpick over insignificant issues, an organization is better off without a performance-improvement program. This is where it pays handsomely to do it right or it costs dearly to do it wrong.

Employees are incredibly perceptive: they can sense if a performance-review process is a paperwork shuffle, a witch-hunt, or a genuine effort to help them enhance their skills and increase their value. It all depends on the attitude of the immediate supervisor and the leadership generally, and how they demonstrate their commitment to the process. Strong leaders care deeply about their staff. They are quick to congratulate employees who make significant progress and show improvement. But they're also diligent about addressing areas of concern before they fester into deeper problems.

Performance Reviews: An Honest Assessment

Performance reviews have always been an important component of our company's human capital strategy. In addition to simply assessing how well an employee performs his or her normal job duties, the performance review process can also be used to create a behavioral profile of the employee and examine how much progress he or she has made toward achieving specific and measurable goals. Additionally, the performance-review meeting itself provides a great opportunity for a supervisor to discuss the employee's long-term career goals and development, which can enhance the employee's current role or prepare the person for a different position.

In order for the process to succeed, supervisors must establish honest, realistic expectations and provide constructive, sincere feedback. Giving feedback is a delicate art. Everyone loves to receive praise, but it's harder to confront unpleasant truths about one's job performance—and just as hard for bosses to dish out that negative feedback. It can be tempting for supervisors to avoid honest discussions about an employee's shortcomings. However, doing this is harmful to everyone—the supervisor, the organization, and the employee. In order for your people to have the chance to improve, they need an honest, accurate evaluation of their performance—the bad as well as the good.

Moreover, don't forget that feedback should be tied to goals. Evaluate progress made on previously established goals (if any), and use this opportunity to create new goals for the coming year (or quarter, or month, etc.). Supervisors should try to align each individual's goals with the company's objectives. Providing annual incentives that reward employees for their individual contributions is an effective way of linking personal accomplishment with organizational success.

Goal setting is something of an art unto itself, and managers often err by articulating goals that are vague or undefined. Years ago, I learned real goals had to have seven characteristics. In order for a goal to be meaningful and achievable, it has to be **personal** (meaningful to you—not someone else); **challenging** (not easily attainable—just out of reach, but not out of sight); **written** (reducing to writing crystalizes thoughts); **specific** (clearly articulate the who, what, why, where, when, and how); **measurable** (a quantifiable benchmark or qualitative description as a determinant of success); with a **deadline** (a goal should have a date for completion) and a **plan to review** (periodic measurement will help determine if you are on track or need to make mid-course corrections).

Throughout my business career, I've used these seven factors to set personal and company goals. In my experience, the likelihood of achievement goes way up using this framework. Find a framework that works for you, and help you and your people set meaningful goals. It's amazing how much momentum your business can gain from this process.

To supplement our own performance-review process, we have our employees undergo an annual self review. This gives them an opportunity to rate themselves and allows the supervisor to compare those self-ratings with the supervisor's perception of the individual's performance. In this way, the supervisor and employee can work toward closing any gaps. Although the formal review may happen annually, giving positive and/or constructive feedback to employees needs to be ongoing. This way the annual review can be an opportunity to look at progress over the longer term and will not be full of surprises.

Benefits of Training and Development

Training and development go hand in hand with the performance-improvement strategy. Organizations that invest in training enjoy higher employee satisfaction and retention rates along with improved productivity and customer satisfaction. Obviously, training and developing your people—bolstering their existing skills and teaching them new ones—has an auspicious effect on your bottom line and helps you maintain a competitive advantage.

At the same time, you must be selective in your approach—when resources are limited, investing in the *right* training that closely aligns with the desired business goals is critical. Training, of course, comes with a cost, both direct and indirect. Direct costs are the expense of training itself, which might also include travel, lodging, registration, etc. Indirect costs are incurred from the loss of productivity from taking employees away from their regular duties. There might also be a "morale" cost for employees who have to pick up the extra slack or feel excluded while their colleagues are undergoing training. If your training program is wisely designed, then these costs pay for themselves over the long term, but it does underscore the need for a prudently planned development strategy that invests limited resources where they will have the most impact.

The investment in training and development is an important part of the company's commitment to the individual employee. Employees are more likely to value a company that furnishes opportunities to enhance their skills and acquire knowledge and experience that helps them advance. On the other hand, employers can also craft elaborate training programs and still experience employee turnover. This is often the case with companies that just offer training for the sake of it and don't align it with the individual's needs and business goals.

At Insperity, we are big believers in equipping employees to succeed. We are not investing in training—we are investing in our people. Employees can see very clearly the commitment we are making to help them be the best they can be, and they reciprocate in their commitment to continuous improvement. We strive to be a learning organization, where commitment to getting better every day is ingrained in the organization. A learning organization is a more capable, agile, and confident company.

Employees who are confident in their roles within the company— because they've received the right training and have the support and resources to help them in their jobs—are more engaged and perform better, which translates into higher productivity, which in turn stimulates revenue growth.

Additionally, as I discussed in the last chapter, training minimizes the risk of employer-related liabilities. Providing workplace training to educate against harassment or discrimination minimizes the occurrence of such incidents and put employees at ease, because they know how to handle these delicate matters. And the mere existence of such training provides a strong defense for business leaders and the company against the ever-present threat of lawsuits. In addition, a training program that truly demonstrates your commitment to your people lowers the risk of employees responding to conflict with legal action.

Techniques for Effective Training

Like many things in business, implementing an effective training and development program is easier said than done. Everyone understands its value, but few really know how to go about putting it together. Obviously, your training must conform to the specific needs of your business, but in working with thousands of client companies over more than three decades (as of 2018), we've found that the following five-step method will work well in almost any organization:

1. **Consider your business goals**. What are you striving for as an organization, and what do your people need to achieve that?

2. **Talk to employees**. Find out *their* career goals, and consider how they intersect with yours. Build the training course(s) around these points of intersection.

3. **Determine readiness**. An employee might have the potential to take on more responsibility at some point, but the person's desire, skills, and experience may indicate that he or she is not yet ready. Have faith in and challenge your workforce, but don't overload them with too much too soon.

4. **Consider various types of learning**. Formal classroom education, online courses, outside lecturers, coaching, stretch assignments—your options abound. Stretch assign-

ments involve assigning an employee to a project that will put his or her abilities to the test, providing a chance to flex both intellectual and creative muscles. Such assignments are good for people who thrive on challenges (and, incidentally, those are generally the kind of employees you want to have working for you).

In-house experts are also a valuable source of knowledge—members of your own staff who can teach others. Mentoring is another wellspring of professional development. Mentoring works best when it's a long-term relationship. It can be greatly rewarding when, over time, the "mentee" cultivates sufficient expertise to begin mentoring someone else, thus creating multiple "generations" of tutelage and shared expertise.

5. **Accountability**. Don't merely train; make sure it's working for all stakeholders. Establish goals, evaluate progress, and provide opportunities for employees to demonstrate what they have learned.

Trends in Training and Development

Traditional forms of training have typically involved companies bringing in outside instructors to train staff or sending staff to an offsite training event or seminar. The internet has transformed how people learn and online, self-paced training experiences offer an effective way for employees to take courses at their convenience, directly from their computers. This delivery approach not only minimizes travel costs, but it also allows employees to participate at their own pace and still provides time for the completion of daily work.

Other online courses can function more like a traditional classroom with an instructor, with the convenience of digital transmission via a web-collaboration program instead of in person. For example, Insperity has a "virtual learning center" that delivers live instructor-led compliance training to our clients. When training is properly designed for online delivery and facilitated by highly skilled virtual presenters, it can be as engaging and effective as traditional classroom delivery, while saving on travel time and expenses.

Learning management systems have enhanced training and development programs while providing a more centralized, streamlined interface. In conjunction with an employee information system, all of a company's training can be managed from one point of reference. Employees can schedule and launch the training from one location, class registration can be automated, and supervisors can track and view reports on training. For example, if everyone in the office is required to take a harassment-prevention course, the system can track who is registered and report when each participant has completed the course. Business leaders can also create training plans for groups or individuals based on key business initiatives or each performer's individual development plan created during the performance-review process. A learning-management system can help employees better manage expectations by clearly defining what needs to be done to fulfill compliance requirements.

While online training offers many advantages, face-to-face, instructor-led training may be preferable in some cases. Leadership development, for example, is an area that's better conducted via traditional in-person training. Emerging leaders need an opportunity to practice new skills, enjoy support and feedback, build relationships with peers, and ask questions. In many cases, a blend of online content delivery with face-to-face follow-up can be an efficient means to achieving desired training outcomes.

Design Training Around Business Goals

One of the biggest misconceptions business leaders have about training and development is that it alone can solve the company's problems. Training is the solution to problems caused by a lack of knowledge or skill, but training *cannot* solve problems caused by misalignment in expectations, direction, resources, and/or consequences for performance.

A common scenario is leadership picking and choosing training programs based only on what they want to see happen in the company, regardless of whether it reflects what the company *needs* at the time. The best approach to dealing with performance problems is to begin with a targeted needs analysis to define performance gaps and identify the causes of poor performance before pursuing any solution. A combination of both training and non-training solutions is usually needed to achieve the desired improvement.

For example, if your company isn't hitting its revenue growth targets because of delays in processing sales orders, what's causing the delay? If employees know how to process orders but the order system is broken, no amount of training will improve performance (and you'll waste a lot of time and effort in the process.) However, if employees aren't completing orders—or are making routine errors that cause rework and delay—you may need to reestablish expectations for accuracy and completeness, improve support tools designed to reduce errors, and then train for any knowledge or skill gaps.

Before we devise a training program for a client company, we meet with leadership to carefully determine the underlying performance issues. Then we can diagnose where and what kind of training will be effective. *Again, training and development in and of themselves aren't going to solve an organization's problems. Development is designed to improve the competencies that can bring about the change that's needed.*

When an organization suffers from lack of engagement, it's often caused by a lack of understanding about what employees are doing and how it ties into the greater good of the organization.

When an organization suffers from lack of engagement, it's often caused by a lack of understanding about what employees are doing and how it ties into the greater good of the organization. Training helps to provide the link between an individual employee and everyone else: here's what I'm doing, and here's why my work helps my department achieve our objectives, which benefits the company as a whole.

Consider the company's goals and determine the skills and competencies key performers need to develop in order to reach them. Every employee should have an individualized plan that includes training and development to help achieve his or her objectives. Several factors to consider include:

- What type of skill development can help the organization meet its goals? Depending on the goals you have established for your company, training may include leadership, team building, individual performance, or specific technical skill sets.

- What type of training system should you implement? This may be contingent on job site location(s) or access to/familiarity with online methods of learning.

- What specific developmental aspects are employees seeking or needing? This may require a closer assessment of each employee's potential skills and goals in addition to areas that may need improvement.

Job-Specific Training

Many business leaders have a programmatic approach to training and development, meaning one training program should fit everyone. However, training opportunities should support individual development plans, which are based on the performance review. For example, companies need to have specialized training for new employees, supervisors, and job-specific roles within the company. This may entail mentoring, cross-training, or industry-specific training. It's a more granular, more nuanced approach to professional development. That means, say, instead of picking customer-service courses to improve customer service, business leaders need to look at what specific training employees need to help them on the job. This is another reason why online training can be so powerful—it is often more customizable and personalizable and can thus be more closely tailored to individual employees' needs.

Our company's core values support an environment that elevates high standards, and we support employees who go above and beyond by obtaining certifications in their respective fields. This often involves devoting the time to prepare for a required examination. Upon completion of their certification, corporate employees can earn a bonus of up to two percent of their annual salary.

We also encourage development opportunities outside of the company with a tuition reimbursement program for those who either attend job-related training and seminars or who are working toward a college degree. These types of professional development programs offer a win-win situation, providing advantages for the person and the organization.

Ongoing Coaching From Supervisors

Think about how you would describe the role of your company's supervisors when it comes to performance management. Do they act as disciplinarians, coaches, or advisors? Or would teachers, mentors, or leaders be more accurate descriptions? Have you defined the roles that managers and supervisors should play in the company and provided requisite training for them to perform these functions?

Many business leaders think that when employees are trained, their development is complete. But in fact, a supervisor must take on the role as a coach to help employees improve and extract the most out of their training. Very seldom do workers do better because they're *told* to. Employees improve when their supervisor mentors them, guiding them until they truly understand what it takes to do better. This is true also of your own mentorship of your direct reports. You demonstrate leadership by cultivating their strengths and teaching them how to downplay or overcome their weaknesses, so that, together, you can all move the organization forward.

After the training, feedback is important, as is putting the employees' newfound expertise to the test: give them the chance to perform the new skills and continue guiding them. Learning is an extended process; it doesn't happen overnight. And it rarely happens without support from above.

One Size Doesn't Fit All

One of the big questions in employment these days is navigating generation gaps. In many workplaces, several generations may coexist under the same roof, and each might have radically different ideas about how to get things done.

As one might expect, different training methodologies work better for different age groups. For example, baby boomers tend to prefer instructor-led training while the younger generations of workers enjoy the convenience of online learning. That said, there are exceptions, and a range of preferences can also exist within a single age group, so don't be too quick to paint people with a broad brush.

Regardless of generation or learning style, the most important factor in learning effectiveness is sound instructional design. It's important for employers to gauge their workforce and customize the training programs to meet the needs of different demographics.

Return on Investment

Once you're ready to roll out a training and development initiative, company leaders and supervisors must champion it and take an active role in its execution. Periodic monitoring and feedback to assess programs and employee development is key. And employees must *apply what they have learned* to their everyday jobs. They will be happier and more self-confident when they are able to see their own training in action.

"Learning" and "working" are not distinct or mutually exclusive categories. Learning *is* work, and work is learning. The more opportunities your people have to engage in the former, the better they'll be at the latter. Regardless of what industry you're in, your employees should never stagnate in their personal, professional, and intellectual growth. Because if they're stagnating, your *business* is stagnating. Keep growing and nurturing new talent and cultivating new skills, and you'll soon see the return on your investment.

Thinking Strategically:

1. Before launching a training program, think critically about which skills and competencies your key performers need, and how those needs tie into the long-term goals of the organization. Develop your training program in accordance with those goals.

2. The variety of training and development options (lectures, conferences, stretch assignments, online modules, etc.) can be daunting. You can't do everything, so a well-designed strategy involves carefully selecting what works for your organization. Don't aim for a one-size-fits-all approach; try to address employee needs on a more personal, more granular level, pinpointing which people need what kind of skill development. Online courses can be effective in this regard because they're more customizable and flexible.

3. Performance reviews go hand in hand with training and development, because the review process identifies skills gaps. But don't just train; analyze, reflect, and seek feedback. Use that feedback to tweak your program further, and measure the impact in the next round of performance reviews.

Thinking Systematically:

1. Training and development is not just a matter of bringing in "outside" resources. Use what you already have. On-the-job training, supervisory instruction and mentoring, and in-house lectures by experts on your staff are also effective, and often less costly.

2. Performance management requires goal setting, and goals should be personal, challenging, written, specific, measurable, and with a deadline and a plan to review.

3. Don't just release your newly trained employees "into the wild." Assess the individual and organization-wide impact of the training. And give people a chance to apply what they have learned.

CHAPTER EIGHT

Strategy #6: Employee Administration and HR Technology

TURNING BUREAUCRACY INTO HIGH PERFORMANCE

Time is money, and trying to manage all of the necessary HR-related paperwork at all levels of the company diverts attention from other areas of the business. Unfortunately, being an employer brings a myriad of regularly scheduled business interruptions. Bureaucracy and red tape are a constant time drain, and business leaders find themselves racing against the clock to take care of important HR paperwork on time instead of using their brainpower for more pressing tasks.

Fortunately, we live in an era of unprecedented technological progress, and software can do most of the heavy lifting for us, systematizing and automating tedious administrative tasks. In addition, HR technology allows us to mine and analyze a wealth of data, allowing business leaders to make better human-capital-strategy decisions.

Until recently, sophisticated HR technology systems were only available to big businesses with deep pockets. But the rise of digital technology, and, especially, cloud-based software, has changed this dynamic. Now, companies of any size can benefit from game-changing, high-tech tools to elevate their human capital strategy. Technology is not a panacea, and some entrepreneurs, enticed by flashy new software, rely too heavily on tech to fix their problems. But a well-designed software program that 1) supports your business' intermediate- and long-term strategy, 2) provides the time and resources for implementation of and training in the software, and 3) integrates with your unique culture and vision can pack a powerful punch.

The HR technology in use today used to be a luxury. Today, it's a necessity. As a CEO, you need to understand that if your technology isn't up to par, you're at an immense competitive disadvantage.

Benefits of HR Technology

HR technology often makes the annual wish list for capital spending, but typically moves toward the bottom as other investments are deemed more essential. Many business leaders consider employment administration mundane and purely "tactical" in comparison to other areas. But it's a necessary and strategic part of running a high-performing business—useful for more than just processing time sheets.

Advantages of HR technology include:

- Streamlines and automates many HR administrative tasks and processes, which saves time and money.

- Offers a centralized, enterprise-wide solution to managing all aspects of the company's HR.

- Enables strategic, data-driven decision-making at all levels.

- Reduces liabilities and financial penalties associated with compliance risk.

- Manages and controls labor costs in areas such as overtime.

- Eliminates paper-based HR processes and manual entry.

- Improves accuracy and consistency of processes, which reduces errors and duplication.

- Engages the entire company by providing self-service functions to take care of individual HR-related administrative tasks.

One of the great advancements of HR technology in recent years has been the emergence of cloud computing. Cloud-based solutions have allowed companies to consolidate and manage important human capital information via collaborative web-based applications rather than confining data to the company's servers or individual computers in the HR department (or, worse, in ream upon ream of paperwork in long-forgotten basement filing cabinets.)

Cloud computing has given rise to the "software as a service (SaaS)" model, which entails a broad range of cloud-based human capital applications to automate HR tasks such as talent management, time and attendance, expense management, organizational planning, training, and performance management. I actually prefer a twist on the SaaS approach that I call "software *with* a service." Software takes care of the grunt work (namely, automated processes that computers perform better than humans), while people provide expert service with a human touch. Sophisticated HR technology is really only as good as the people who are using it, so you need people who can extract the full range of its features and benefits.

One of the most quantifiable advantages of HR technology systems are the significant time and labor cost savings. For example, a study conducted by the American Payroll Association showed that manually processing employee timecards takes an average of six minutes per card, per pay period. In contrast, organizations with automated time and attendance solutions achieved 12 percent greater workforce capacity utilization than those with manual time and attendance processes, according to a recent Aberdeen Group study. When companies are paying employees for every second they're working, business leaders want to maximize this precious time.

HR technology can also make certain decision-making processes easier and more efficient. For example, some software programs aid compensation management by aggregating and analyzing various sources of employee-performance data that managers would otherwise have to manually comb through to determine employee salaries.

Performance management technology supports setting goals and expectations, and it has revolutionized the old "annual performance review" process by providing an ongoing feedback loop between supervisors and employees throughout the year. This produces more accurate, timely data, to the advantage of both supervisors and employees, who tend to appreciate more regular feedback.

One of the greatest strengths of good HR technology is the positive impact it can have on employee morale, engagement, and retention. In today's competitive workplace, employees can and will judge a company based on its workforce-technology experience. This is especially true of the millennial generation and younger employees who have come of age in the era of the internet, social media, and smartphones. A company that invests in HR technology is demonstrating its ongoing commitment to making the workday easier and more convenient for its employees, replacing time-consuming administrative tasks with efficient, user-friendly digital solutions. In this way, your technology strategy is not just administrative or transactional; it forms a part of your organizational culture.

As an example, think of the much-maligned onboarding process, which is a new employee's first introduction to the company. A company that makes its new hires spend hours on cumbersome paperwork is sending a different message than a business that conducts interactive onboarding and benefits enrollment online. Employees will feel valued when leaders have taken steps to make life easier for them and help them quickly acclimate to the organization. At Insperity, our online onboarding process has cut the amount of time spent on paperwork by 60 percent.

One of the highlights of current HR technology is the "self-service" model, where users (i.e. employees) can perform simple HR tasks themselves instead of having to go through HR staff. With the ability to access, update, and manage their personal information, employees can find the information they need when they need it. HR personnel also benefit from self-service technology because it means they spend less time doing paperwork or answering employees' routine questions.

Enterprise-Wide HR Technology Solutions

An ideal integrated HR solution will encompass all facets of a company's HR practice, including recruitment, onboarding, employee administration, payroll, benefits, talent and performance management, learning, career development, messaging, and role-specific workflows. Referred to as a human capital management system, such platforms offer strategic decision-making tools to HR leadership and the C-suite through the use of customized analytics to evaluate hiring, budgeting, performance, and compensation trends. Enterprise-wide HR technology generally works best when it consolidates data into a single, centralized database, which is one of the chief advantages an enterprise-wide HCM system has over a point solution.

One of the challenges larger companies face is when different divisions produce too many siloes of data, resulting in waste, inefficiency, and duplication. Consider the cumbersome process for handling paperwork for a new employee. Basic personal information (date of birth, address, etc.) is submitted and entered into a spreadsheet in one department. Then that employee's benefits information is entered and maintained in another database either in-house or via a third-party. Payroll information is stored on yet another database or possibly via another system managed by a different vendor. Later, the employee's performance review will be administered and maintained by a paper-based system, and so on.

Anytime a new hire is brought on or an employee makes changes to their personal information, each of these separate systems has to be updated. Not only is this an inefficient way of managing important information, there's no method to use technology to strategically evaluate the employee's role, compensation and performance, career development, or advancement opportunities over the course of his or her tenure. An HCM platform eliminates all these siloes by centralizing all data in one place.

An all-inclusive, enterprise-wide HCM application is a longer-term investment that provides more data to work with for year-over-year trend reporting and pre- and post-organizational-change analysis. If reducing manual data input, duplication, and human error is your goal, centralized, all-inclusive platforms beat out the à la carte solutions. HCMs tend to be costlier, though over time, they may actually be less expensive since they're less burdensome to maintain and upgrade than a basket of point solutions. An HCM platform is also more scalable—as your business grows, it can grow with it.

At Insperity, we've developed an HCM Technology Platform that gives employees 24/7 access to the tools and resources they need: viewing paystubs, enrolling in and managing their benefits, tracking retirement plans, submitting time sheets, checking their vacation allotment, and more. Employees can also access training and development courses at their convenience, and supervisors can track progress.

A robust HCM platform has workflow built into the software, which helps employees follow important steps in processes that ensure accuracy and limit liability. This can include approvals in the hiring, enrollment, performance-management processes, or cost-saving steps toward getting time keeping and payroll right.

Another advantage of Insperity HCM technology is the capability to encourage collaboration and communication between supervisors and our HR experts. Features like a "click to chat" allow for immediate support as supervisors deal with daily HR issues.

Even with all of the conveniences that technology offers, it's important for companies to maintain a personal touch. Technology should be considered an extension of a company's human services, not a replacement for people. Taking care of, say, performance reviews online is convenient, but it shouldn't be an outright substitute for the personal interaction that should occur between a supervisor and employee.

It's just a matter of striking the right balance and figuring out what works for you and your people.

HR Technology Point Solutions/Websites/Apps

If you are not quite ready for a full HCM solution, there are "point" solutions options for small- and medium-sized businesses or even websites and apps to address specific HR needs. In contrast to comprehensive, organization-wide human capital software services, these solutions offer support in specific areas, such as recruiting, payroll, performance management, and employment screening.

One example of where point solutions can be useful is with recruiting. The marketplace is full of technology solutions helping businesses find the right employees and employees find the right jobs. These solutions can find the best candidates for specific positions by searching hundreds or thousands of resumes based on certain search criteria, eliminating the burden of sifting through stacks of resumes. If a candidate's skills match the employer's needs, the employer can filter applicants further by administering questionnaires and tests online.

And all of the recruiting information for a specific job can also be stored and managed for future use, avoiding duplication of data management. No more keying in the same person's name five times in five different applications: that information is now stored in one easily navigable, centralized database.

Sometimes a specific HR need is so intense, a point solution is the answer. Here's an example of how time and attendance technology solutions were the necessary first steps in deploying HR technology. A large retail client that employed several thousand employees in multiple business locations kept track of employees' hours via a manual time-keeping system. The company's store, department, and regional managers were spending hours each week going through thousands of employee time sheets. Not only were they manually reviewing, but they also had to "slice and dice" different allocations of time each employee spent on specific tasks. Then, paper reports had to be created and faxed to the corporate office for re-keying. In short, the system was bloated, outdated, and frustrating for everyone involved.

The company decided to transfer its paper-based system to a cloud-based time and attendance solution, and the payroll process went from many hours of HR effort to less than thirty minutes each week. Instead of relying on humans to pool paperwork from multiple, far-flung stores, the company could dump it all automatically into one centralized hub that seamlessly interfaced with the company's payroll system. An added bonus of the new system was that with more accurate, more granular data, the company could use the system's reports for real-time labor budgeting.

This kind of problem is not confined to payroll administration; it's a challenge in all areas of HR where processes and approvals are administered via an inefficient paper-based system, or even by a computerized system that's out of date. It emphasizes why the right point technology, combined with the right processes and the right people to oversee them, can dramatically reduce HR workload and improve productivity at multiple levels of the organization.

One drawback of point solutions: when you start combining several software packages, your company's HR technology program can become a confusing patchwork of different vendors. This, in turn, might require greater technical sophistication to bridge the gaps between systems. And if your business grows significantly in the next few years, the à la carte approach is not as easily scalable as an all-in-one strategy. That's why enterprise-wide human capital management systems are often preferable.

Self-Service Options

Self-service is another exciting trend in HR technology. Companies have found that many routine HR inquiries or tasks normally handled by HR staff, such as answering questions about someone's PTO balance or enrolling someone in benefits, can be done by the employees themselves, using user-friendly interfaces accessible at work, on one's home computer, or on mobile devices. Employees tend to like self-service solutions because it gives them more control and allows them to get the information they want, when they want it—without having to pop in to the HR department or spend five minutes on hold with the help line.

Self-service platforms can be customized in different ways depending on what level of self-service you wish to provide managers and employees. There are usually different "tiers" of access for different personnel groups; for example, managers generally have access beyond the basics: including compensation data, performance reviews, and tracking of employee training and development.

Some business owners are hesitant to offer self-service because they are concerned about employees having too much control over potentially sensitive data or even abusing that information. Fortunately, there are ways of handling these concerns, at the process level as well as the technological level. For example, if an employee updates his or her mailing address, a person in HR can be notified to check for accuracy before the information is saved in the database.

Choosing the Right HR Technology Platform

HR technology's application to SMBs is best understood considering the three layers of HR we discussed in chapter two. The administrative, transaction-driven layer is where HR technology should shoulder the most burden. The more HR technology you can deploy to help with this layer, the more you will control your risk as an employer. Even with the best HR technology, it will take people using it correctly to optimize results. The second layer is a process/event-driven layer: someone gets hired, someone gets fired, someone gets promoted, someone enrolls in the insurance plan, etc. This layer requires a good balance between technology and expertise to be effective. The top layer is the strategic or outcome-driven layer; HR technology can help here, but it will take real HR consultative services to realize your big-picture, long-term business goals.

Software with a Service

The further you go up these layers, the more it takes real HR consulting experience to achieve the outcome you want. In other words, to really extract a strategic benefit from software, you can't just "plug and play." You need an expert who knows how to utilize it.

Before investing in HR technology, companies need to consider these five factors:

1. What are the most critical pain points you are trying to address? Keep your eye on these and don't get caught up in the bells and whistles that look great, but you will never use.

2. Consider your company capabilities in implementing and maximizing the benefit of new technology. Make sure you have someone on your team that can champion the selection and implementation process.

3. Realize new technology will most likely result in new processes. Don't get stuck trying to make the technology fit exactly how you do things today.

4. Make sure you only consider companies with a track record— ones that will still be around when you need them. There are many new entrants in the business that come and go, and you don't want to get stuck with technology and no support.

5. Make sure you evaluate technology with a "software with a service" mind-set. The technology will not produce the desired outcome by itself. Consider whether you should invest some additional HR expertise as you invest in the technology.

Naturally, technology can be expensive, so you must consider the cost carefully. Don't just calculate the licensing fees. Ancillary costs, such as the expense of updating and maintaining technology and hiring additional IT staff, are also a budgetary burden. For example, some business leaders may think that there's a considerable cost savings to building a custom database, but the amount of time, expertise, and manpower required usually exceeds the expense of licensing a SaaS application.

But even with licensed software, tread carefully, read the fine print, and look at all the costs involved: licensed software may initially offer a less expensive alternative, but costs for server licenses, operating systems, upgrades, data backup, support, and disaster recovery can add up. As a general rule, SaaS costs are more predictable and cost-effective over the long term in comparison to licensed software.

The process of choosing what's right for you doesn't have to be complicated. Before making a decision about what to buy or license, figure out what you really *need*. What aspects of your current HR technology infrastructure cause the most headaches? What are you doing every day, week, and month that seems like a waste of time? Also consider the positive—what are you doing well? (If it ain't broke …)

Think of which tasks the company should automate, divide your wish list between pressing needs and would-be-nice-to-have "wants," determine your budget, and figure out who will be making the decisions about your HR technology acquisitions. Ideally, it shouldn't be just one or two people handling the task. Assemble a vendor/software-selection committee comprised of key stakeholders. Most importantly, don't rush the decision. Software is a long-term investment, and making a hasty choice, only to find once the new technology is installed that it doesn't suit your needs, can prove to be a costly setback.

Technology and Culture

Technology forms a big part of your business' culture. Use it to shape the kind of workplace you want to create. That doesn't mean your company must be a state-of-the-art, cutting-edge technological visionary (unless, of course, that's the brand you're pursuing). It just means that technology makes an impression on employees and shapes how they feel about their employer. It also communicates something about the leadership and its commitment to progress and change.

The little things go a long way when it comes to technology's impact on your people. If you can spare them a little bit of tedium by replacing monotonous administrative tasks with a rapid, digital alternative, it makes people feel better about working there. It strengthens their loyalty and their confidence in the organization.

Technology is also an effective means of promoting certain cultural values that contribute to a positive workplace. Teamwork, camaraderie, friendship, innovation—these qualities can be encouraged through intra-company apps or social networks that facilitate connections between colleagues and reward "points" for completion of tasks or for making progress on certain goals—call it the gamification of HR. And I'm not talking about "business goals," but the kind of interpersonal and emotional goals on which a healthy culture is based.

Here's a simple example: during our Hurricane Harvey relief efforts to help people clean-up and recover, we created a Facebook group for Insperity employees. That group became the social/ volunteer hub of this exciting, fulfilling project. Through the group, people organized activities, talked to one another, met urgent needs, and generally fed off one another's energy in a way that was vibrant, powerful, and uplifting. It was, simply, fun.

To be clear: these trends don't mean that every CEO of a small- or medium-sized firm has to do hurricane relief or design "HR games" just to have an effective HR technology strategy. Those things aren't goals unto themselves; they're just tactics that may or may not be appropriate for your particular business objectives. Just keep in mind HR tech applied to your business can also add to the fun. Never underestimate the productive value of fun.

Also understand that while technology enhances the culture, it must grow organically *out* of the culture. You can't magically fill culture gaps with an app. For example, if you want to develop wellness as a component of the culture, it's not sufficient to just add a wellness feature on the employee portal and wait for it to catch on. What you do technologically must be congruent with who you are as an organization.

If your HR strategy is only concerned with compliance data and back-office processes, you're missing an incredible wealth of human capital power that produces engaged, aligned, and inspired employees. Use it for the prosaic, grunt-work stuff, but also use it to unleash the spirit and energy of your people. That's what effective human capital management is all about.

Thinking Strategically:

1. It's a simple rule, so it's amazing that so many CEOs ignore it: your technology program must be congruent with your broader strategy. Every piece of software and hardware you license or purchase should have strategic value—should be oriented toward accomplishing some long-term goal. If not, ask yourself if you really need it.

2. HR technology should also fit with the company culture. Different types of workers prefer interfacing with different technology—or no technology at all, in some cases. The generation gap between employees can make this difference especially pronounced. Technology should exist to serve the employees, not the other way around, so fit your strategy to the characteristics of your workforce, and use it to unchain their esprit de corps.

3.   HR technology does more than make rote tasks easier through automation—it creates an entirely new set of tools, such as data analytics and decision support, that you need in order to remain strategically competitive in the twenty-first century economy.

Thinking Systematically:

1.   Implementing new technology can be hassle-free (especially with the support of a good third-party vendor), but it's not always a simple matter of "plug-and-play" and off you go. Sometimes, you have to adjust your internal processes to make it work. As you remake your technology program, think about which old processes need to be modified or eliminated for the technology to do its job.

2.   Point solutions are useful for targeting specific needs; enterprise-wide HCM systems offer a more centralized, all-in-one approach. Sometimes, the former is all you need; in other cases (especially in larger and more complex organizations), a centralized solution might be more apt. Your choice should depend in part on the expected growth of the company—if you think you'll add a hundred people to your roster in the next five or ten years, a scalable HCM system is probably a better choice.

3.   Self-service has changed the face of the HR function in many forward-thinking companies. It might not *replace* the old way of doings things, but it is here to stay. Consider whether and how self-service technologies can benefit your organization. When done right, they offer advantages for

all parties involved: boosting efficiency, relieving HR staff of their routine administrative workload, and providing a new tool for employees to quickly obtain the service or information they need.

CHAPTER NINE

Strategy #7: Human Capital and Mergers and Acquisitions

LOOK BEFORE YOU LEAP

Investing in a private company is a little like getting engaged. Before you pop the question, you want to know everything (okay, *almost* everything) about your soon-to-be spouse, so you can be assured there won't be any unwelcome surprises en route to a strong, loving, lifelong partnership. After all, private-equity investment is, like a marriage, a long-term commitment, with a lot at stake for both parties. The last thing a starry-eyed newlywed wants to discover once the honeymoon is over is that the new spouse has some devastating secret or major problem that's been kept hidden. You need to know what you're getting into.

This chapter looks at the human capital implications of buying—or selling—a company, whether it's a wholesale acquisition or a part-ownership deal. It's an important topic because it's a frequently over-looked area of transactional risk. Investors or business owners who are contemplating buying or selling a stake of the business always scrutinize the conventional measures of a company's health: its financial statements, its customer list, its growth projections, its risk profile, its capital structure. Those who dig deeper might also look at other aspects, such as the company's technological assets, or the background of its CEO. But when it comes to considering the *people* who make up the business, very rarely do investors look beyond the few executives at the top, and that's a mistake, because they can't accurately assess the valuation of a company without understanding how things work every day at ground level.

In other words, they're looking at the output of the business, but not how that output is actually generated. They're not considering the human capital side of things, which is the best way to determine whether the company will be profitable over the long run or is a disaster waiting to happen.

What do the day-to-day mechanics of the workplace look like? What are the people doing and how well are they doing it? Are they in the right jobs? Are they satisfied? Are there visionary leaders guiding them—and are they liked and respected by their subordinates? What is the culture like? What are the performance, recruitment, and training protocols?

All of the critical elements we've been discussing thus far in this book should be part of your due diligence when you're thinking of plunking capital to buy a company, merging with another firm, or even participating in a joint venture.

Caveat Emptor: Let the Buyer Beware

Insperity helps investors avoid pitfalls by appraising a company's human capital situation. Private companies, especially smaller ones, tend to be tight-lipped about their inner workings, so it's not so easy to take a good long look under the hood. Uncovering that blind spot is one of our niche areas of expertise.

When prospective investors forgo the human capital part of their research, their initial investment thesis is a little too rosy. Maybe the numbers are promising, and the CEO has a stellar track record. But once the deal is signed and these investors get in and see for themselves how the company operates on the day-to-day, human scale, all the (potentially fatal) flaws start to emerge. Now, instead of popping the champagne in celebration, they have to go back to square one and fix all these human capital issues: misaligned leadership, a problematic culture, disconnect between individual motives and corporate objectives, etc.

You see this especially with young companies that look good on paper but haven't really developed a proper human capital "infrastructure." They get hot and draw the attention of venture capital. Maybe the upstart firm is even generating lavish profits or sitting on a gold mine of an idea. But because the company is so young and underdeveloped, its inner workings are still a mess, despite its outward attractiveness. That doesn't necessarily mean it's a bad deal, or that these problems can't be remedied. But that reality must be priced into the investment thesis.

Sellers Beware, Too

Naturally, these principles also apply on the other side of the negotiating table—to the owner of a company looking to attract investors or to sell the company outright. The market value of your business can be greatly enhanced by its human capital management. Even if the picture is good on the outside—if the numbers are strong and the company has a solid reputation in the industry—you can't paper over human capital shortcomings forever. If something is rotten on the inside, it's going to be rotten on the outside. And the buyers of your company are going to find out sooner or later.

The drawback of this situation goes beyond discouraging investors or downgrading the valuation of your company. It's also a matter of how much control you'll be able to retain once you bring other owners on board. For executives who intend to remain majority or part owners, your future role will be determined in large part by how well you manage your people. If your new partners come in and find that the HR/administrative management is in disarray, they're going to muscle in and demand changes—and that could mean you'll be forced to relinquish some of your decision-making prerogative.

Don't give your future partners an excuse to sideline you from managing your own company. Fix any human capital problems now, before they're exposed to prying eyes.

The Business Alignment Survey

To help investors and business owners, we use a diagnostic tool we call the "business alignment survey." It's a time-tested way to manage risk, improve productivity, and assess alignment between all the moving parts of an organization—providing a snapshot of a company's human capital outlook that covers everything from communication and how decisions are made, to how promotions are doled out and how workers are compensated.

The process starts with a half-hour phone call to discuss the general structure of the organization and determine which members of the leadership team will participate in the online survey. The survey questions themselves are straightforward, and most can be answered with a simple "yes" or "no"—things like: "Does the company set performance goals for each employee?" "Does the company conduct exit interviews?" "Does the company have a documented succession program for key positions?" And so on.

Then, we analyze the data to produce a report that includes graphical depictions of alignment/misalignment among organizational levels, departments and locations, an assessment of regulatory risk and civil risk, and proficiency measures of the organization's foundational, optimal, and strategic human capital practices.[4]

Sample Survey Results
Alignment
Business alignment survey results
Does the company set performance goals for each employee?

```
                            CEO
   ┌──────────┬──────────┬──────────┬──────────┐
Product      Client    Marketing    Sales    Finance and
development  services                        admistration
   │          │          │          │          │
Engineering  Call center  Inside   Business    Accounting
                                   development
                                      team
   │          │          │          │          │
   QA        Account     Outside   Inside sales   Legal
             management
                                      │          │
                                   Channel sales   HR
                                                  │
                                                  IT
```

■ Yes ■ No ■ Uncertain ■ No answer

___

4   "The Insperity Business Alignment Survey," Insperity MidMarket Solutions, accessed November 6, 2018, http://www.insperity.com/wp-content/uploads/2015/07/BASflyer_WEB.pdf.

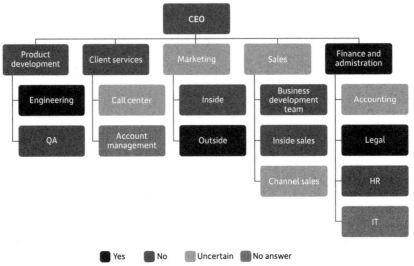

Misalignment
Business alignment survey results
Does the company link employee performance to strategic (growth) planning?

During the business alignment analysis, we leave no stone unturned. In addition to the survey, we conduct on-site research in which we examine personnel files, financial reports and other documents, conduct interviews with the executive team, and sometimes administer an employee survey as well. For example, one thing we look at closely is the compensation system and benchmark the compensation against the market rate. As an investor, a compensation system that's out of whack—too stingy, overly generous, or seemingly random and arbitrary—is a red flag. That's a problem that's going to affect the bottom line one way or another.

One of the biggest reasons mergers and acquisitions fail is cultural fit. The reality is that change of ownership and combining with another organization is one of the biggest upsets that can happen in a company, and, of course, change is one of the most disruptive factors in human behavior. Having a clear picture of cultural differences between two organizations combining or even between a venture capital firm and the target acquisition can provide an important indication of future success. Change causes anxiety, and anxiety causes a loss of confidence, which erodes trust. Trust is the cornerstone of individual and group performance and directly effects the speed of execution of company plans. A thorough evaluation of the cultures coming together can highlight areas of commonality that can be emphasized and areas of divergences that can be reconciled. An upfront, honest approach and discussion of expected cultural change when an investment transaction takes place is a far better way to begin the new relationship.

By understanding human capital from every angle, we provide a fresh set of eyes to comprehend how the work is getting done at the people level and determine if there's a better way to do it. So, if you're a business leader who wants to make the company more attractive to investors, or an investor who wants a full audit of the strengths and weaknesses of a prospective acquisition, the alignment survey has tremendous value.

Investors tend to be very shrewd people with a keen eye for a good deal and an instinct for spotting potential pitfalls. But even the savviest investors tend to be limited in their understanding of human capital and how it really keeps the gears of great companies turning.

Whether you're selling a company you've built yourself or looking to acquire a stake in one before it grows into the next big thing, you need to accurately, thoroughly, and candidly assess the quality of its human capital management.

Thinking Strategically:

1.   Just as owners tend to overlook human capital in favor of the other core areas of business, investors disregard human

capital management in their risk-reward assessment, at their own peril. Don't leap before you look.

2. Once again, everything comes down to alignment. If there's a lack of synergy among the leadership when it comes to goals, it lessens the firm's value in the eyes of investors.

Thinking Systematically:

1. Insperity's business-alignment survey uses a proven methodology to peek under the hood of a small- or medium-sized firm, so you don't have to come up with your own method or figure out which questions to ask, and to whom.

2. If you're an owner looking for outside investors, fix your human capital problems first. It will strengthen your negotiating hand and bolster your status as a leader in the eyes of partners—after all, if you can manage your people well, then you can manage your business well.

CHAPTER TEN

Strategy #8: Organization and Leadership

LEAD BY SERVING OTHERS

In 2000, Insperity experienced the most severe challenge in the company's history—a true moment of reckoning for its leadership. But by sticking to our principles and being willing to change and adapt, we came out better than ever. The crisis ended up being a blessing in disguise.

One of Insperity's central service offerings to our small- and medium-sized client companies is access to a comprehensive benefits plan. For many years, Insperity relied on one carrier to provide all of its health insurance benefits, which were contracted with the carrier in a manner similar to other large employers. The expected cost for the plan was factored into the price of Insperity's service fees charged to clients. For this reason, the carrier was contracted, as a fiduciary, to provide timely and accurate claims information necessary for Insperity to price its services in a way that allowed us to remain profitable.

However, a crisis struck when the insurance provider stopped holding up its end of the agreement and failed in its fiduciary capacity to provide accurate, timely claims data. Then, they arbitrarily raised Insperity's premiums retroactively! Suddenly, we were faced with the prospect of having to pay out millions of dollars from our own coffers. This is a really big problem for any company, but a nightmare for a public company. We were left with few choices, none of them good: ultimately we had to pay them, leave them, and sue them. No matter what, someone was going to incur a huge loss—either us, or our clients.

Our leadership had a major decision to make, but in my view it wasn't a difficult one. Thousands of SMBs had placed their faith and confidence in us to provide services to them under our one-year contracts. Under these highly unusual circumstances, we could've gone back to our clients and simply explained the situation and raised our prices to cover the loss. However, we decided that just because the large insurance company had violated its contract with us was no reason for *us* to break our contract with our clients.

As a result, we took a major financial hit that cost the company in excess of $25 million, wiping out our profitability for 2002. The company's stock price plunged from previous highs of $43 per share to $1.99, which reduced the company's market capitalization from more than $1 billion to less than $60 million.

This was a devastating lesson, but it ultimately provided tremendous value to the company's organization and leadership development. Our actions demonstrated our management team's commitment to the company's high standards and its core values (integrity, respect, accountability). In the end, our decision boiled down to doing the right thing. What started as a crisis became, in the end, a way of proving our mettle, and a testament to the value of our service offering and our clients' continued confidence and trust in our relationship.

As any successful entrepreneur can tell you, adversity can serve as a great litmus test for a business and its leaders. It can either highlight the best qualities of leadership and the organization, or its worst. In order for an organization to survive difficult times, leaders must be willing to conduct honest assessments of themselves and the company, and to make tough choices and difficult changes accordingly—bending, so as not to break.

Executive Team Alignment

Successful organizations are led by strong, united management teams. A business can't advance when the leadership isn't in tune with the organization's overall goals and objectives. It's amazing how many leadership teams aren't all on the same page regarding the company's mission, values, and vision, when that should be the starting point.

One way we help our client companies tighten the alignment gap is through the business-alignment survey I talked about in the previous chapter. The diagnostic survey provides a candid look at leadership alignment on human capital strategy and growth objectives. Surprisingly, almost 99 percent of the time, the survey results uncover a misalignment in the leadership. Leaders are surprised to learn that not everyone is in sync with respect to their understanding of the organization's mission and core values, short- and long-term objectives, and the key success factors that drive the results.

Leadership gaps sometimes become pronounced when client companies acquire a new business. For example, a long-term client company acquired a similar business that was struggling during an economic downturn. On paper, the acquired company was in good shape—it had a great client base and a solid reputation. However, our client struggled with the unwieldy task of merging two leadership teams.

We worked closely with the client to help them assess the best leadership alignment strategy going forward: would the new company be somehow integrated into the parent company, would it operate independently, or was there something special about the acquired firm's leadership style that our client would adapt to the parent company?

We brought in both leadership teams to conduct a strategy session to work out this conundrum. The client company's CEO revealed that he especially liked one of the core values of the acquired company, but his own company didn't have the processes in place to execute it. The answer was simply to incorporate the already established system of the acquired business into the parent company's processes.

Engaging all parties in this challenging, but revelatory, dialogue forced them to think about the critical issues, identify dissonance between leadership teams and styles, and then determine how to maximize and blend the strengths of both entities to help them achieve their goals: a win-win, best-of-both-worlds resolution.

Ensuring that each leader is held accountable for his or her individual teams' performance while remaining aligned with the company's overall goals and objectives sometimes requires cross-communication between different groups within the organization. Understandably, this can produce major rifts. When sizable gaps exist between company leaders, that discord is reflected in the rest of the organization.

However, that does not mean you should pack the ranks of upper management with people who think exactly like you. On the contrary:

look for people who bring skills and perspectives that you lack. You need people you respect and with whom you work well, but they should *complement* you too. "Alignment" does not simply mean "emulation."

When Insperity first began, my business partner and I recognized that we needed to surround ourselves with leaders who could balance our strengths and weaknesses. One of the essential qualities of running a business is to have the self-awareness to recognize what you excel at and what isn't your forte. Nobody's good at everything. Moreover, a strength, if taken to an extreme, can become a weakness. For an example, "go-getters" are valued in the business world, but I'm sure we've all met people whose zealous "go-getterness" runs so unchecked that they just trample over everyone and alienate their allies.

I've always been an effective starter, innovator, and developer, but I'm not a natural "completer." Those traits have served me well running Insperity, but I couldn't have gotten to this point without having talented completers in my corner to carry things to the end— people who, unlike me, are natural closers, proficient in grinding out that last 20 percent of a task or project needed to bring it into being. Building a team of people who allow your unique strengths to flourish while neutralizing your weak spots is essential to achieving alignment at the top level.

One of the best ways we maintain alignment within our management team is by regularly participating in off-site retreats. These retreats help keep us all on the same page and moving in the right direction. They allow us to get away and work *on* the business instead of *in* the business. The off-site location gives us a fresh perspective to look at things from the outside. It's not always smooth sailing; sometimes tension arises as we work through our differences and hammer out an accord. But at the end of the day we respect and support one another, which allows us to make decisions that are in the best interests of the company.

I've also seen companies do these retreats the wrong way. It's not just enough to show up and go through the motions. First, set an agenda that is meaningful and that will generate enthusiasm among participants. Have the other managers in attendance "own" part of that agenda, too, so they're playing a leadership role rather than merely being passive attendees. After all, the goal is alignment, and that means teamwork, collaboration, harmony; not just "the boss" talking to (or at) a room full of direct reports who are counting down the minutes until they can get back onto the golf course.

Another way to make retreats work is to provide an opportunity for people to vent a little bit. That too is part of the process. In fact, one measure of a leadership team's cohesion is the ability to voice disagreement and dissent amicably and productively. It's okay if things get heated, as long as people are respectful. *Then* everyone can go out and hit the links (or some other scheduled diversion), cool off, and resume work later, safe in the understanding that we're all in this together.

Just don't forget that the work doesn't end with the retreat. Achieving alignment isn't a one-time task; it's an exercise that requires constant maintenance and attention.

Adopting the Right Leadership Style

Leadership style and philosophy are important elements of a human capital strategy. Don't conflate "leadership" and "management." They're related, but distinct. Budgets, resources, inventory, and costs should be *managed*. The function of leadership is to guide, support, and inspire the people, the organization's most valuable assets.

Deciding upon a leadership style sets a standard for the higher-ups to exemplify and for employees to emulate.

Leadership styles span a spectrum from authoritarian to collaborative, and leaders should choose the style that's best suited for advancing their organization. Once you've chosen a style, hone it. Tailor it to your particular needs and circumstances. Amplify its strengths and minimize its weaknesses. And don't be afraid to enlist the assistance of a leadership coach, who can provide the outside perspective and the pinpoint guidance that can develop your own leadership skills.

Servant Leadership

The style we practice at Insperity is servant leadership. Over time, servant leadership has become a central part of our company's culture, so much so that it's something that employees, regardless of their position, often model. In fact, a recent corporate employee survey revealed that more than 90 percent of employees agreed that they're responsible for demonstrating servant leadership qualities at work.

Servant leadership turns the conventional notion of leadership on its head; instead of a top-down orientation, the people at the top work for the benefit of everyone else, from the bottom on up. It's based on inspiring people to work to achieve individual and company goals. Rather than relying on coercion, the goal of servant leadership is to empower our employees by giving them the freedom and flexibility to work well, innovate, and advance without fear.

Jerry always wanted to make sure that everyone felt safe to fail, which is part of learning and part of any healthy corporate atmosphere. He understood that being afraid is harmful to workplace culture, and he didn't want anyone to be fearful of making a mistake. I agreed with this concept, with the caveat that if we fail, we should "fail fast," learning from our mistakes and expeditiously moving ahead. Trial and error is a proven method in business, but if it occurs slowly, the organization will suffer. Over the years, "fail fast" has become an important mantra in our culture.

Beyond that, our version of servant leadership is based on the following six principles:

1. **Being leaders rather than managers.** Now, there's nothing wrong with managing. Good management is an essential part of a well-run organization. Company heads should be skilled at both leading and managing. But leadership is something distinct from management. It is the skill of influencing people to work enthusiastically toward common goals and for the common good.

2. **Relying on authority rather than power.** Power is using your might or position to compel someone to do something he or she might not otherwise do. It is implicitly coercive. Authority is more of a skill rather than a blunt exercise of force. It means getting people to willingly and even eagerly do what you want, because your relationship with them confers some degree of personal influence.

   That's the key word, really: *relationship*. Cultivating healthy relationships is a great source of authority because it means the people who work for you *want* to contribute and aren't just acting because of the fear of getting disciplined, or fired.

   Power benefits only the few, the elite, the ones who *hold* power. Authority benefits everyone.

3. **Using inspiration rather than motivation.** Motivation can be a powerful driver of behavior. But motivation is a

"carrot and the stick" mechanism. It's a more "animalistic" way of getting people to act, reducing one's impetus for doing things to the threat of punishment (the stick) or the promise of reward (the carrot).

Inspiration is a better method, and one that is more conducive to servant leadership. Inspiration relies on understanding and support to motivate people. Helping people understand the sum total of their life experiences; understand their capabilities, their inclinations, their desires, and their capacity for mounting the obstacles in front of them. In short, helping them discover their *calling*. That's inspiration, and that's what servant leaders should create.

4. **Cultivating commitment over cooperation.** Cooperation is obviously beneficial, but its power is limited. It's temporary and shallow. Cooperation is, "Hey, can you help me move this table?" Commitment is long-term and deep. It's more sustainable. It relies on good relationships built over time.

The way you lead determines whether your people are merely cooperative, or whether they're *committed*. Cooperation is good for achieving simple tasks. But the big-picture items, the grand vision, the innovative thinking that truly great companies seek—you'll need commitment for that.

The key to commitment is reciprocity. It's a two-way street. If you demonstrate your commitment to the people who are following you, they in turn will commit to you and to the success of the organization.

5. **Listening vs. caring.** For managers, for leaders—for everyone—the importance of listening is self-evident. It's a valuable business and interpersonal skill. Really, no collective human endeavor can function without it. But *caring* is something else entirely.

Listening results in understanding, but caring results in a relationship, and relationships are what will carry you further as a leader. Listening is focused on the other's problem, but caring is focused on the other person. Caring is the reason behind *why* you're listening: what you seek to understand, what you want to do with the information.

Listening establishes communication, that's a good thing, but caring establishes a connection and that's a nobler objective to which servant leaders should strive. Don't just listen. Care.

6. **Optimism vs. faith.** This one's a bit tricky, since these two values may seem synonymous, but they're in fact quite different. Optimism hopes for the best, where faith takes action in expectation of a specific outcome. Optimism looks for good from others; faith *sees* the good in others. "I believe in you" are powerful words out of the mouth of a leader. They mean, "I believe you've got the commitment, I believe that you have the skills, I believe you have the capability, and I'm going to help you."

That's faith. And when you have faith in others, others have faith in you, too.

At Insperity, we extol both optimism and faith. In fact, one of our core values is "looking to the future with an abiding faith and optimism." Faith attempts and achieves what no one else believed possible. Optimism creates a positive environment, but faith creates a sense of purpose, a sense of calling, a sense of mission that's powerful and inspires action toward achieving objectives.

Discretionary Effort: An Outcome of Effective Leadership

Servant leadership makes people want to work hard not because they *have* to, but because they *get* to. That synergistic energy produces discretionary effort, and that's a big part of what leadership is all about. It means your people are genuinely enthusiastic to come to work. They're not just there to draw a paycheck. Their heart's in it, and they're in it for each other. When you're not around, and an emergency strikes, or plans go awry, good leaders can rest assured, knowing that their people are going to get the job done—going above and beyond if necessary, and doing whatever it takes.

I recently saw this in action when we brought on the largest client in our firm's history. We had to do so in a very compressed time line, and given the client company's size, there were a number of unique complexities that made it an especially difficult project, requiring collaboration among several Insperity departments.

In other words, a tall order. Was it time to crack the whip? No, of course not—servant leaders don't have one. They don't need it.

Ultimately, everyone came together and did their part, completing the transition of the new company before the deadline. They came up with a number of "out of the box" solutions, because they were free to be creative and get the job done. When you've built a company that's powered by discretionary effort, you see people rise to the occasion time and again. It makes all the headache of running a business worth it, because it's undeniable proof that you've created something more than just a profit-generating organization. You've enabled people to reach their potential and be their best selves.

How to Rebuild Trust after a Failed Leader's Exit

It's easy to talk about the positive impact of leadership when things are going well. But sometimes, leaders flame out. This can have a devastating impact on employee trust, morale, and productivity. Worse, the problem doesn't necessarily end when an incompetent or corrupt leader is forced out. Often, he or she leaves behind an atmosphere of resentment and mistrust, and that individual's replacement is now charged with winning people over. It's a formidable task.

If you're the one replacing a failed leader, you'll have your work cut out for you, but you can smooth the transition by following certain guidelines.

The foremost challenge is regaining people's trust. Whether you're an outsider brought in from another firm or someone who has been promoted from within the company, you'll have to prove yourself to your new team. That means understanding what (and whom) you're working with. What are their talents, attitudes, and perspectives? Find out by opening a direct line of communication and encouraging a continual, two-way discussion between you and your subordinates.

Second, ask questions. Find out from your people what went wrong with the previous leader, and learn from your predecessor's mistakes. Practice "active listening"—not just passively taking in complaints but cultivating a healthy dialogue and giving immediate feedback. This demonstrates that you're focused and you're taking to heart what your employees are telling you.

In the process of letting employees air grievances, there's a risk that the conversation will be subsumed by negativity and bitterness, especially if the previous leader's tenure was particularly contentious. As the new leader, it's important that you temper this negativity. For jilted employees, private, one-on-one conversations are a good pressure valve to supplement the public talks. This way, they can express themselves freely, without judgment, in a safe place. Ask them what they'd like to see changed. If there's another manager these disgruntled employees trust, you can invite him or her to participate in the conversation too. Then ask them to put the past behind and for a fresh start.

Failed leadership is a serious problem, but it doesn't have to turn into a full-blown crisis. When the situation is managed deftly by a leader who listens, cares, and acts decisively, you can put the problem to bed and return to focusing on what you and your team do best.

Organizing for Success

One of the most important responsibilities of leadership is to determine the best organizational structure for your company. The goal is to establish a structure of roles and responsibilities for individuals and work groups that will best support the company goals and increase the likelihood, degree, and ease of success. How you organize your people feeds directly into how decisions are made and how effectively people collaborate across the company. These two factors are very important in driving the "speed of execution" in your company. Poor or slow decision making bogs down the whole organization. Organizing your people ineffectively also determines how intuitive it is to set goals at the individual and work group level that directly result in achieving the company wide objectives.

Most businesses are traditionally organized around one of the following factors:

1. **Function:** This is the most typical, logical structure, especially for small organizations. This is simply establishing work groups around the major purposes and tasks like sales, operations, finance, etc. This basis is internally focused on determining roles and responsibilities.

2. **Geographic:** This approach groups employees based on their location and proximity emphasizing the need for direct supervision over functional priorities. The focus here is efficiency of the local operating unit.

3. **Product or Process:** This method determines roles and responsibilities using the ultimate product or service delivered by the company or the processes necessary to optimize the offering as the main priority. This emphasizes the need for design, development, testing, etc.

4. **Customer:** This technique prioritizes the customer experience as the basis for determining roles and responsibilities. This can be based on either the life cycle of the customer from prospect to former customer or by demographics around customer types.

5. **Matrix:** This practice uses a combination of factors above in establishing roles and responsibilities recognizing competing priorities. For example, you may have geographic locations operating as a unit but centralized functional support.

All of these approaches have their usefulness and application, but in today's environment of information overload, constant communication, and mobility, leaders should consider some other factors. Technology has dramatically increased the velocity of business and introduced new ways for employees to interact and collaborate. Consider organizing around an objective you have or key success factor critical to your company.

One of the outcomes from the company crisis I referred to earlier in this chapter was reorganizing Insperity starting with the end in mind. Our crisis clearly drove home the need for matching price and cost for our services in order to achieve both growth and profitability goals. But like many companies, pricing was in the sales organization because it was part of the sales function and integral to the process of bringing on customers. Cost management, on the other hand, required negotiating insurance contracts and managing benefit programs and payroll taxes. This group seemed logically segregated in the administrative part of the organization far from the sales process. Our experience with our insurance carrier (I am talking about the severe beating we took) inspired some "out of the box" thinking on how we should organize the teams to achieve the results we wanted.

Once the pain subsided, we formed the "Gross Profit Enhancement" division and we brought together all the people, processes, and tools we needed to take full responsibility for the matching of price and cost for our services. The goal of this team was imbedded in the name of the division, and everyone on the team knew their reason for existence. This group was formed with the responsibility for a critical success factor clearly visible in the financial statements of the company. Since we organized around this major objective, our success in this area has been incredible. Once again, the power of alignment is demonstrable.

Cumbersome organizational structure plagued by communication obstacles and confusion over decision-making processes can thwart even the best business plans. Many companies are not organized effectively—their structure stymies growth, efficiency, and cooperation between people and departments, or employees and managers are not properly aligned. We've found that cracks especially begin to surface in organizations when they hit the mid-market range, around 150 employees. At this juncture, they often experience a disconnect between the owner/CEO and employees, a decline in revenue, and a dip in employee retention. It's critical for leadership to periodically review the organizational structure to address whether it allows the company to meet its goals.

First, diagnose the problem correctly. It's natural to want to place the blame on people when things aren't working. Look at the processes. Are they enabling people to get the job done, or are they getting in the way? Is there a better way to do things? If it's not a process issue, then look at the organization. Are you organized in such a way that lets people act and allows processes to flow unimpeded? If not, is it time to restructure the company?

Here are a few common red flags that indicate that a structural/organizational overhaul is in order:

- If goals aren't being met (or employees are simply working too hard to achieve those goals), then leadership needs to assess the situation. It's counterproductive for employees to work too much overtime or to have to muscle through complexities to do their job.

- Are there frequent and severe clashes between different departments or divisions?

- Is the group unclear on its function and how it feeds into the overall corporate goals and game plan? For example, if leadership doesn't understand why a department or group chose a certain course of action, it's time to ask why that department wasn't aware they had better options.

- Leadership should determine which groups should work closely together and which functions need separation. What are the common goals that would unify different divisions or work groups within the company?

- Is the company unable to move quickly, or does it lack the agility to take advantage of market opportunities? Sometimes conflicting functions or goals between two divisions impede both divisions. Organizing the company's departments by business activity is sometimes an effective remedy.

- Sudden loss of key talent or clients is a major indicator that something isn't working right in the organization.

We have had many examples where some of these symptoms appeared and an organizational change provided the solution. An effective change in how you organize your team can really lift the lid on your performance. We were struggling with a problem I have referred to over the years as our success penalty. We grew very fast serving small businesses within our original target market of less than 100 employees. Over time we found our services really worked helping clients succeed and they grew right out of our target into the mid-market space with several hundred or more employees. Many of these companies thought they outgrew our model and took the HR function in-house, leaving us with the need to replace them with many more small accounts. We suffered a penalty in our growth rate from successfully serving our clients.

We worked hard to improve our service to larger customers and made some progress within the service organization structure in place. However, these clients were more complex and needed more interaction at higher levels in the organization. Too many issues had to be treated as exceptions and we were having to apply too many resources and simply work too hard to achieve the results we wanted. Serving these clients with the same processes and service team model designed for our small business customers was like trying to fit a square peg in a round hole.

We reorganized into three segments based upon customer demographics. We added our emerging growth segment for clients with 100 to 150 employees recognizing the unique needs of these fast growing customers that were transitioning from small to midsized. We established a mid-market division for our clients with more than 150 employees and began to develop a customized service model to meet the needs of this underserved segment of the marketplace. Over time we not only began to retain larger customers, but we also began selling customers in this space and even accounts with thousands of employees. Organizing the teams effectively added tremendous value to the company and improved our service to all three segments.

Organizing with the end in mind can be transformational. Achieving success in the mid-market space doubled our addressable market, and our success penalty has become a premium to our growth rate instead of a drag.

Leadership and Organization

One of the most important tasks of leadership is to organize the company to enable employees to achieve the company mission. The role of leadership is to create an environment where people can flourish individually and collectively within the specific work group or team they are on, and as a part of the organization as a whole. Leaders go beyond casting the vision providing the goals, roles, rules, and tools to give employees the greatest opportunity to be successful. Leaders also provide the underpinning of core values guiding decision-making and demonstrating their application in day-to-day situations.

When Insperity was in the throes of the crisis I talked about earlier, our leadership followed the company's core values of maintaining integrity, accountability, and perseverance—and sticking to our mission. If an organization has a shrewd strategy, a well-designed structure, and alignment between its top people and its chief objectives, it can weather any storm.

Each business is unique, and each entrepreneur running it is naturally inclined to a certain leadership style. But the most successful leaders recognize that by lifting up everyone, they lift themselves up too: creating relationships, instead of creating fear; commending, not commanding; inspiring, not intimidating; being authoritative, rather than authoritarian. That's how you build something great, something people are excited and proud to be part of. That's how you set an example for your employees, your clients, for the world at large.

Thinking Strategically:

1. Without organizational alignment, you won't get far. The top people will be stepping on each other's toes, and progress will be stymied by disparate ideas about the company's vision. Take a step back, have an honest discussion with key people, and reassess the direction you want to go.

2. Structural problems can be tricky to diagnose, since "structure" is an all-encompassing quality, and sometimes it's hard to tease out structure from other factors, like people or processes. If your business is faltering, is the problem in the organization, or something else? Some things (interdepartmental disputes, a dip in retention rates, etc.) are telltale signs that it's time for a restructuring.

3. Effective leadership requires a coherent leadership style, and that style must be custom-fit to your unique business. For us, servant leadership has worked well as a unifying philosophy. And remember, leadership is not just for the leaders—in a healthy organization, *everyone* exhibits qualities of leadership.

Thinking Systematically:

1. Misalignment has many causes; poor communication might be the biggest. Foster more robust, regular, and systematic dialogue with other leaders. Organize an annual retreat to reconnect with one another and iron out the wrinkles.

2. Failed leadership is destructive and disruptive. The new leader who comes in must work quickly to rebuild the trust that has been lost. Again, good communication (active listening plus caring) is key to achieving that.

3. Times of crisis are when a company, its leaders, and its values are really put to the test. Don't compromise your values; instead, be flexible with other aspects. Shake up the organization's structure as needed, or reconfigure the leadership team. You're likely to emerge from the crisis stronger than ever.

CHAPTER ELEVEN

Strategy #9: Employee Communications

KEEP THE DOOR OPEN

Communication is the lifeblood of any relationship. If communication is healthy, it can build trust and loyalty. When poorly handled or nonexistent, it can wreak havoc.

Most companies develop strategic communication plans for their external customers while neglecting their *internal* customers: the employees, who as a group are its most important investment. The goal of an effective employee-communications strategy is to cultivate a pattern of information sharing that builds trust, confidence, and mutual respect among employees on a daily basis. The fast rate and sheer magnitude of change that occurs in business today makes this element of your human capital strategy more important than ever.

For business leaders, good communication is a matter of "painting the picture." That means being clear with employees about what they're being asked to do and why, how their role is important within the framework of the organization, and what is the game plan for the following weeks, months, and years. Don't keep people in the dark; bring them into the light. The more you can share with them, the more likely it is they'll contribute discretionary effort in pursuit of the mission.

Link to Company Culture

The best way leaders can grow the culture they want is to talk to employees about it at every opportunity. Mission and value statements are only as good as they are communicated. Simply creating a mission and values statement isn't enough—employees need to be reminded of them and the important role they play in their daily interactions.

A client company of ours—a 700-employee, heavy-industrial engineering/infrastructure subsidiary—was struggling with leadership-alignment problems. Leaders' responses on the business-alignment survey varied nearly 100 percent of the time, indicating severe misalignment when it came to the firm's human capital strategy.

One of the survey questions was "Does the company have a mission statement?" to which the CEO and almost everyone else answered yes. Only the CFO answered differently. He had put down "uncertain."

During the post-survey debriefing, when the CEO saw the CFO's response next to the near-unanimous "yeses" of the rest of the leadership group, he got angry. In a flash, the CEO marched out of our presentation, grabbed the mission statement off the wall in the lobby, brought it back to the conference room, and slammed it on the table.

"What does this look like?" he spat. "It's the mission statement!"

The CFO calmly looked at the CEO and said, "If you're asking me if we have two paragraphs filled with words most of our employees don't use, then yes, we have a mission statement. But do our employees understand our mission, and can they tie it to what they do each and every day? I answered 'uncertain' because I don't think they can, and our productivity metrics confirm it."

The room grew quiet as everyone pondered the undeniable truth of the CFO's words. The company had a mission statement, but the mission statement itself wasn't the problem. The problem was communication. The mission statement may as well not have existed.

A company's culture should guide the tone of all communications. Before we started Insperity, my business partner and I were determined to make sure that our management team walked the walk by doing what we said we were going to do. We meant this not only for the way we wanted to serve our clients, but also for our relationships with employees. "Integrity," "respect," and "perseverance" are values that we practice from the moment we enter the office to the moment we leave (and, I like to think, in the intervening hours, as well). In turn, employees also practice these attributes in their personal interaction with their coworkers, clients, and prospects.

That's just good leadership—if you live it, others will follow suit.

The greatest communications plan in the world will backfire if employees don't trust the company's leadership. Employees have a keen sense of when leaders are speaking from the heart or concealing something.

One way we've continued to build our company's culture as our organization has expanded over the years is through Insperity's award-winning intranet. In addition to delivering important company news, it is eminently useful for highlighting the important contributions employees have made throughout the organization. From recognizing quarterly award winners to running features on individual employees, our intranet has kept employees connected to each other and informed.

Be Strategic and Consistent

What are your reasons for communicating with employees? Are you trying to build trust or promote the exchange of ideas? Is it to open dialogue between employees and management? Or is the purpose to educate employees about the business model or update them on internal developments? Whatever the reason, business leaders need to establish the intent, which may include several objectives and involve different approaches.

Emotions affect employee performance. When employees are feeling anxious or upset, negativity creeps in and hampers productivity. Over the years, our management team has striven to maintain emotional stability in employees through a consistent communications strategy. Once we determine the messaging and how we plan to communicate it, we stick with it and repeat it as often as possible. This approach has helped us to build and maintain a positive, enthusiastic environment.

Employee communications should be a stabilizing factor in the organization. Employees need to be lifted up, not pushed down, especially during difficult times. And that also necessitates some measure of regularity in terms of how often you communicate with them. If they become used to a certain style and volume of communications, and then that dialogue suddenly stops, it creates a sense of emotional unease. That kind of uncertainty is toxic to productivity and morale.

The best way to avoid this is to continue to provide a steady flow of communication.

Especially in large and geographically diffuse organizations, business leaders are confronted with the ongoing challenge of making sure everyone is on the same page. For example, our service organization is one of the largest departments at Insperity, totaling more than a thousand employees at four different service centers and over seventy local offices in the United States. These employees are on the frontline and serve our clients on a daily basis, and they need to be kept well informed of any changes that may affect our clients.

Consequently, our service organization has established a formal communications process to ensure that our service teams quickly and reliably receive the latest information. Our executive vice president of service operations formed our Service Operations Leadership Team, which meets for two days twice a month with our general managers and field operations leaders to review important information and changes that need to be communicated to our teams. This forum gives these field operations leaders an opportunity to ask questions on behalf of their staff. We want our supervisors to be equipped to answer questions from our service providers, who need to know the "hows" and "whys" so they can serve our clients. This communications chain has been a very effective way for us to manage information among the service providers and build trust between our leadership and service teams.

Our corporate sales staff has also been tasked with keeping our sales teams informed and up to date on the latest developments in the company and the industry at large. Fortunately, technology makes it possible to maintain open communication with more than 500 field sales professionals in over seventy offices scattered throughout the United States. For example, through a monthly podcast, our regional sales managers, executive vice president of sales and marketing, and other leaders within the organization remain in close contact with the sales teams and provide them with the information they need to do their jobs well.

This podcast works so well because the lines of communication run both ways: an interactive call-in segment provides our field sales professionals an opportunity to ask questions and share practical insight and experiences from the trenches. This call-in segment is also a chance for outstanding individuals to be recognized for their efforts in front of their peers and supervisors. That recognition has the ancillary benefit of motivating others and creating a bit of friendly competition.

It's also worth mentioning that the act of listening to the program has become an act of team bonding unto itself. It's not just individuals sitting alone at their desks with headphones on. Instead, the staff of each sales office typically listen in together during these broadcasts.

In essence, the program is effective because it provides a national voice so that everyone hears the same message, learns vital information in a timely manner, and gains a better understanding of best practices from their peers, thus strengthening the ties that bind our vast sales organization.

Face-To-Face Communication

One of our most effective methods for communicating with employees is our quarterly all-employee company meetings. These were established as monthly meetings during Insperity's humble beginnings, when our entire staff could fit into a small conference room. As our company has grown, we've leveraged the long-distance reach of the internet to broadcast these meetings to our other locations to ensure all employees can take part. The purpose, however, remains unchanged, as these meetings provide employees with a much-needed opportunity to hear directly from the company's leadership. It's also a time to celebrate the winners of our quarterly and annual employee awards.

Personal communication has played a key role in managing and motivating our national sales force. As our company began to expand into different markets, our leadership wanted to make sure that our sales team was still connected to our corporate team. One way we try to support our sales team is by bringing them all to Houston for our annual sales convention to provide them the latest information, training sessions, and new or revised marketing tools for the upcoming year. This convention concludes with a formal awards banquet to honor outstanding individual and group performers from the previous year—with the highlight being our coveted Circle of Excellence award winners who, along with their spouses, join us for a weeklong, all-expenses-paid destination trip.

This face-to-face time with our sales team has provided much-needed motivation to help our sales force meet company goals, form stronger interpersonal bonds with other people in the organization, and celebrate our corporate culture and our unity as a 3,100-person strong company.

We also run a special program for new employees called i2i (Introduction to Insperity), where we invite them to corporate headquarters to talk about the culture and history of Insperity and to start building relationships we hope will last years or decades. A leader from each part of the company comes to speak, putting a name with a face and a face with each department, which makes new employees feel like they matter. The i2i experience is so worthwhile because people come out of it feeling that they're a vital, appreciated part of a vast organization.

These examples demonstrate that as powerful and convenient the internet is as a communication medium, nothing can replace the emotional value and motivational power of real human interaction.

Soliciting Feedback

Organizational communication only works if it runs bottom to top as well as top to bottom. While employees need to hear key messages from management, they also need opportunities to provide feedback. And sometimes that can be a very difficult thing to do, because we leaders may not always like what we hear. But we must listen to employees' concerns in order to alleviate them. It's also a fact that employees possess a unique and valuable perspective. They're sometimes aware of things happening "on the ground" that even conscientious, deeply involved leaders might be blind to. By listening to employees, the concerns they share today could spare the company from a crisis tomorrow.

We have always promoted an open-door policy for employees to speak with anyone, and that includes providing a forum for employees to ask questions of upper management. Prior to each of our company meetings, employees submit questions or concerns (anonymously, if they choose to do so). As CEO, these questions have always allowed me to keep a finger on the pulse of the organization and gauge any areas of concern or anxiety. I enjoy addressing them in the company meeting so all employees get the benefit of the answers. It's important for employees to have an outlet to express themselves without any fear of retribution. Often, the most challenging questions are the most helpful, allowing us to explain issues and put rumors to rest. On that note, when it comes to dialoguing with employees, don't speculate, or dwell on uncertainties—only communicate what you *know*—and explain that up front. It is also okay to answer some questions, "I don't know" or "We are still working on that." Honest answers like those help to build trust.

Unfortunately, as a public company, there are times when we can't divulge confidential information to employees. But we work very hard to be open, transparent, and forthcoming about everything, including problem areas and sources of concern. While we might not have all the answers all the time, we do our best to explain our decisions, and we have found that to be the most effective way to communicate with our people.

At the start of chapter ten, I talked about how we were able to survive one of the company's direst challenges. A big part of that was because of how we communicated with our workforce during that trying time, when we made every effort to keep them informed. Our policy of open and honest dialogue enabled them to continue to work hard, persevere, and maintain their faith in the company's future. This two-way trust and respect that has been built over the years provided the strong support that allowed us to continue to fight the good fight, and it ultimately reshaped our organization for the better.

Thinking Strategically:

1. Communication is part of any entrepreneurial endeavor, but different situations demand different communication styles. Think about what you're trying to achieve (build trust, stimulate innovation, reinforce compliance with company norms, cultivate loyalty?), and tailor your message and medium to that goal.

2. Emotion—don't think of it as touchy-feely stuff that's irrelevant to the business world or to a professional setting. On

the contrary, emotion is a central part of strategic employee communication. Craft a reliable, even-toned, honest communication policy that creates a sense of emotional stability in the organization. How you regularly talk to employees has a big impact on how he or she feels at work.

3. Strategically effective communication runs both ways: from management to the workforce, and from the workforce to management. Candid, open dialogue and a culture of sharing (feelings, information, ideas) benefit all parties.

Thinking Systematically:

1. Consider which communication resources you have at your disposal. Digital methods (podcasts, online newsletters, good old-fashioned email) harness the instantaneous reach of online and mobile communications. But "analog" methods (face-to-face meetings, retreats, conferences) are invaluable even in a high-tech age, especially when you want to cultivate personal relationships and trust between individuals and teams.

2. Devise a method for employees to convey feedback. Ideally, or at least in certain situations, it should be anonymous, so they can speak freely. Sometimes, a lot of good can come from a tough question an employee might not be willing to ask on the record. Respond to these anonymous questions openly to demonstrate that you're taking their feedback seriously and acting on it.

CHAPTER TWELVE

Bonus Strategy #10: Faith at Work

Conventional management theory posits that organizational initiatives succeed when upper management supports them. A human capital strategy is no different—it requires championing by leaders to grow and prosper. That championing goes beyond just providing the necessary material and logistical support: it requires an unswerving belief in the mission.

In small- and medium-sized organizations, there's no replacement for the firm conviction of the owner, entrepreneur, or CEO when it comes to facing challenges and leading important campaigns. Employees are continually and carefully looking into the eyes and weighing the words of the company's leaders to assess the sincerity of that conviction. Employees have a finely honed intuition for quickly determining whether a new initiative is an idea-of-the-month or a real change that's going to happen.

Call it "entrepreneurial faith." It usually starts with an initial sudden urge to start a new business—what has been referred to as an entrepreneurial "seizure." It's the rush of unexplainable optimism about the future that's motivated by more than just a personal desire for wealth. There's something else that electrifies the dream and churns inside the dreamer—the tantalizing prospect of creating something from nothing en route to building an enterprise (or an empire).

Some of the world's most successful businesses have been started and led by individuals with a sense of calling and purpose; they had a cause that drove them to risk everything and dive in. They believed in themselves. And they *needed* that faith. Because that belief propelled them to keep moving forward in the face of tremendous obstacles in order to succeed.

From Optimism to Faith

For most entrepreneurs, the ball starts rolling with the initial excitement that comes from an idea for a product, service, or a new enterprise. Once the idea is fleshed out a bit, more thought is invested until the entrepreneur starts to acquire a real sense of optimism about what might happen when this inchoate concept is developed.

In time, in spite of the occasional seed of doubt (often planted by a skeptical friend or family member), this optimism grows and becomes more targeted and specific, turning into genuine hope for success. The entrepreneur dares to permit himself or herself to think, "Wow, this thing is really going to happen!"

But hope alone is not enough to overcome the challenges of starting a business. You need resolve and determination to push through distractions, limitations, and unforeseen problems. Competitors and regulators will stand in your way, as will the subtle negativity of those who may be jealous of or threatened by your success.

Ultimately, hope must be nurtured and developed into a deep and unwavering conviction with a power of its own. This occurs by gaining confidence and belief in your product or service, your people and your culture, and your overarching vision. Your resolve increases as you acquire business acumen and skills, the kind of skills that only come from *doing*. Your newfound confidence is the fuel that keeps you going.

In time, your entrepreneurial conviction becomes a creative force to solve problems, overcome obstacles, and persevere when most others would give up the fight. The best word that fully describes this attitude, resolve, and the action that it inspires is *faith*. I've seen it many times, in many settings: a creative force that drives entrepreneurs and creates great business leaders by turning optimism into hope, and transforms potential into real, concrete results.

I'm an emphatically optimistic person, *and* a person of faith. Both qualities served me well in establishing the company, and they still serve me well every day of my life. Recall that as we discussed in chapter ten, the terms "optimism" and "faith" are related, but they're not interchangeable. Optimism "hopes for" a successful outcome; faith expects and acts on it, even in the darkest days. Optimism makes for a positive environment, but faith creates a true calling and a unifying sense of purpose.

Faith at Work Defined

Acting and speaking out of this deep sense of conviction about what the future holds has the effect of raising the expectations of others. It can draw others into the vision by creating buy-in, which inspires discretionary effort and steadfast dedication to a common cause.

This type of faith is contagious, and others will come to share the conviction and commitment it takes to do great things. A sense of mission with a clear vision, coupled with a sound strategy and tactical plan, are the core ingredients of success. But the catalyst of it all, the bright spark that gives it life, is faith.

Faith to Overcome

At Insperity, we've faced many obstacles over the years that at times seemed insurmountable. Sometimes the problem was a lack of capital or cash flow. I specifically recall one such crisis during our early years. After a period of steady growth, we suddenly needed to acquire a large capital deposit for the workers' compensation policy that covers our client companies' employees. This coverage was a core component of our service to our clients, and if we had no policy, we would have been unable to meet our contractual obligations to our clients. In other words, we would have been out of business.

So, faced with the prospect of having to shut our doors, we worked tirelessly and cast a wide net in search of additional growth capital. We were astonished as the deadline approached, and one after another possibility for financing fell through. In a short time, Jerry and I went from thinking we would be able to choose a suitable funding option from a handful of suitors, to staring despondently at each other from across the table, clean out of options, and with fewer than forty-eight hours on the clock before our policy expired.

But Jerry and I kept our faith in the face of this adversity. We knew we had not come this far just to be shut down by a deposit requirement on an insurance policy. We believed in what we were doing for small- and medium-sized companies, and we believed in how we were helping employees and their families by providing big-company benefits in the small-business community.

Even so, we needed a miracle.

While Jerry and I sat glumly in our conference room, coming to grips with the fact that our last financing candidate had officially opted out, a man whom I had never seen before walked in the door. He was the friend of one of our management team members and he needed some financial advice. After receiving a settlement for a considerable sum of money, this man wanted to know what to do with it.

Our colleague called us into the office, and the man then asked a question that amazes me to this day: would we be open to letting him make an investment in our firm?

This seemed too coincidental to be true, so we asked how much he was considering investing. Our jaws dropped when he blurted out the amount, which happened to be the exact amount we needed to pay the deposit on our workers' compensation policy. Flabbergasted, we didn't even ask what the settlement was for until he was about to leave. The answer was the final irony of the situation: he had been awarded money from a workers' compensation settlement!

When we needed a miracle, one walked right through the door!

Faith to Lead

No matter the source of your optimism, hope, confidence, and faith in the future, you can't succeed in business without the faith to lead your organization. This means having faith in yourself—and that doesn't always come naturally. Some entrepreneurs are surprised by the unexpected position of leadership in which they find themselves once their company starts growing. One morning they wake up and realize they're at the forefront of an operation with people analyzing the choices they make and looking to them as the example. This can be a jarringly new and often bewildering experience. But it's just part of an entrepreneur's job.

I will never forget 9/11 for many reasons, and everyone has their own story about where they were and what they were doing that horrific day. What hit me especially hard was that people had been attacked in their workplace, which was a vulnerable target that symbolized the amazing combination of our free enterprise system with the ingenuity and productivity of the American worker. Many of the people who died on that fateful September morning were just ordinary people at or on their way to their jobs.

As the tragedy unfolded, I watched the news as business owners frantically tried to account for their employees and locate survivors. Over the next few weeks, as the nation waited for the dust to settle and struggled to come to grips with the enormity of what had occurred, the job of leading the surviving employees back to work became a formidable challenge unto itself. Business owners and leaders who were directly impacted by the attacks were suddenly thrust into a leadership role well beyond any that they had signed up for. The faith required to pick up the pieces and to look to the future with optimism and hope in the face of such a devastating event drove home the role of business leadership—of the faith to lead. Sometimes, especially in the wake of a tragedy, there is nothing to fall back on but faith.

For all of us, our work life represents a substantial portion of our waking hours; for most people, work is their primary vehicle for accomplishment and self-realization. Day in and day out, the faith to lead people in the workplace does not have the drama or the life-and-death significance of 9/11, but it does carry an unsung importance that holds our society together and makes our country great.

Moving Your Company Forward

Your company is a battalion of soldiers marching forward with a common purpose: to earn profit. Or at least that's the idea. How widely shared is the purpose and how intense is the focus? Any army of soldiers needs a well-thought-out strategy for success. And you need an effective human capital strategy for your company.

This book has endeavored to provide a framework for you to lead your team to success. The road map is complete, but the journey is yours and yours alone to take. A dose of entrepreneurial conviction is all it takes to start. Your vision, your drive, and most importantly your outlook toward the future with an abiding faith and optimism will set the tone for your people to stand by you on this journey.

CHAPTER THIRTEEN

Should We Continue the Conversation?

Companies of all sizes struggle with growth. But small- and medium-sized firms really have their work cut out for them, forced to do more with less while competing with larger companies with seemingly inexhaustible resources. Meanwhile, the smaller firms still have to contend with the same regulatory demands that their larger competitors are better equipped to handle.

Insperity levels the playing field by giving entrepreneurs access to HR and administrative benefits, personnel, and infrastructure of a large company while taking much of the burden of human capital demands off your hands. From payroll processing and timekeeping to complex legal-compliance matters and benefits administration, a Professional Employer Organization (PEO) like Insperity provides the freedom to do what you do best: running and growing a business.

We serve you tactically and strategically as a partner, but like any good partnership, you play an equal role. We're in the business of HR outsourcing, but I think *insourcing* is a more apt term: we provide you unparalleled expertise and essential new capabilities so that you can do your job better.

And we don't just help with the nuts-and-bolts administrative stuff. Insperity also works to achieve alignment between an organization's goals and its HR strategy. We manage our own company by thinking and acting strategically *and* systematically, and we empower you to do the same. If you are convinced of the connection between your people strategy and the success of your company, Insperity has a service offering to come alongside in support.

Workforce Optimization

The crown jewel of our portfolio of services is our Workforce Optimization solution. If you want to move your company ahead as far as you can as fast as possible this comprehensive offering may be the catalyst you need. This service platform is built upon the unique legal construct of co-employment we have perfected over more than thirty years. Through co-employment, your company gains group buying advantages, cost stability, and reduced liability as part of Insperity serving hundreds of thousands of employees in this model. Workforce Optimization is an all-in-one, across-the-board HR service that includes:

- Reliable, accurate payroll and HR administration. We'll take care of the tax records and manage the mountain of paperwork.

- Your choice of a range of Fortune 500-level health insurance and benefits. We have options to fit all types of companies.

- HR-related compliance. This is definitely an area you should delegate to experts. There are simply so many regulations on the books—and they're constantly in flux—that you'll drive yourself crazy and expose yourself to unnecessary risk just to get a handle on them. We'll also help you interface with government agencies to deal with wage claims, I-9 audits, etc.

- Billing that will actually help better understand and manage employee costs.

- Professional, high-touch service. We're not a call center; we're a team of experts who know the HR business inside out and understand your needs. Our HR specialists provide personalized guidance that is as friendly as it is professional.

- Advanced software. Technology evolves so fast that it's hard to keep pace. Moreover, it's hard for business owners to know which HR technologies are worth the cost and which just look good on the showroom floor. We'll help you figure it out.

- Performance-management support. We help you design and execute performance appraisals, provide compensation resources and tools, offer supervisor coaching, and assist with climate surveys.

- Training and development support. We'll give you the resources and guidance you need to implement what works for your people and your business goals.

- Almost any other HR support you may need because through co-employment we actually become your HR department.

Workforce Acceleration

More recently, we have added the most comprehensive traditional employment solution in the marketplace for those not yet ready for the PEO co-employment model but are ready for a step up in efficiency and effectiveness in HR. This solution may be for you if your company is in an earlier stage of your business, on a tight budget, or in a risk category that doesn't qualify for Workforce Optimization. Workforce Acceleration is a comprehensive human capital management and payroll solution with the right blend of Insperity service and award-winning technology which includes:

- Employment Administration, Payroll and Tax Administration.

- Time and Attendance, Employee Onboarding, Training and Development, Performance Management.

- Compliance Support: Affordable Care Act Compliance, Leave Administration.

- HR Resource Center: HR Best Practice Guidance; Self-Service Online Tools, Forms, Resources; On-Demand Training Videos; HR Resource Support.

- Brokered Benefits Management: Benefits Administration, COBRA Administration, Fringe Benefits.

Middle Market Solutions

If your company has more than 150 employees, you are facing all the HR challenges of a big company with the limited resources available to mid-market firms. Insperity is leading the way delivering both co-employment and traditional employment solutions to this underserved market. Your company can have all the advantages of either Workforce Optimization or Workforce Acceleration above with a unique level of customization to meet your specific needs. You will benefit from a dedicated team of mid-market HR experts, plus be assigned an executive sponsor from among our management team.

Since Insperity fits in this category with more than 3,100 corporate employees of our own, we can come along side and help your company become an employer of choice and get on a trajectory of success. We know how to do it, and it's fun!

How to Get Started

We work with all types of companies from very small with as few as five employees to companies with thousands and growing. But it doesn't matter how many employees you have, they are your employees and your company deserves the breadth, depth, and level of care of Insperity services. This is our mantra that has differentiated Insperity in the marketplace.

- The breadth of services we offer is unparalleled. No one does all we do for our clients.

- The depth of our services provide a unique competitive advantage for our clients. What we do behind the scenes is unmatched dealing with some of the most difficult challenges like government compliance and healthcare benefits all while our clients focus on their own profit opportunities.

The level of care we provide comes directly out of our culture and mission to help our heroes—small and mid-size business owners—succeed.

If you're interested, give us a call. We'll get a little more information about your company and what you're looking for in order to connect you with the right business performance advisor. Our business performance advisors are well versed in the challenges faced by SMBs and figuring out how to resolve them. The business performance advisor will conduct a free, hour-long "discovery call" with you to determine what you need and how we can help.

After that, we go through a data- and information-collection process, create a proposal, perform a technology demo if you're looking for technological improvement, and then proceed with the official enrollment of your business as an Insperity partner.

Leading by Example

When we started, we were essentially the only company doing HR insourcing/outsourcing. Today, according to the National Association of Professional Employer Organizations, there are more than 780 PEOs operating in the United States serving 156,000 to 180,000 client companies, so we're no longer the only ones in the game. But I'm confident we do it best. And our record is a testament to that fact.

It's not just our stellar record with client companies that makes me proud. It's also the way we practice what we preach. We've built a business where people are happy to work. We've created a model, an exemplar, a paradigm for what a good people strategy looks like. And we've been able to share that with the world, helping others—entrepreneurs, investors, employees, all stakeholders—share in the positive contribution made possible by the Insperity way.

I hope we can share it with you and help you take care of your people.

FOR MORE INFORMATION PLEASE VISIT
www.PAULSARVADI.com

A Special Offer
from
ForbesBooks

Other publications bring you business news. Subscribing to *Forbes* magazine brings you business knowledge and inspiration you can use to make your mark.

- Insights into important business, financial and social trends
- Profiles of companies and people transforming the business world
- Analysis of game-changing sectors like energy, technology and health care
- Strategies of high-performing entrepreneurs

Your future is in our pages.

To see your discount and subscribe go to Forbesmagazine.com/bookoffer.